Versatile, adaptable, easy to work with and tasty beyond belief, beef is the perfect meat for almost any occasion. It's little wonder that, when we think about what to cook for tonight's family meal or the coming weekend's dinner party, we start with a particular cut of beef in mind then build the rest of the menu around it. All the recipes in this book confirm this premise – with beef as the focal point, the rest of the dinner's planning just seems to fall into place... with imagination and ease and an inimitable yum factor!

Pamela Clark

Food Director

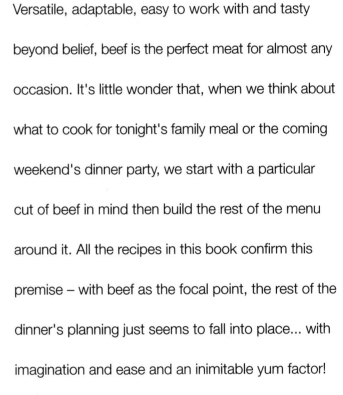

contents

weeknights

No one but the cook of the house knows how difficult weeknight dinners can be: you don't have much time, your family expects a different dish every night and you have to make something that will please everyone. This chapter's tempting selection of recipes will provide you with a repertoire of fuss-free but delicious main meals.

herbed porterhouse with roasted kipfler wedges

PREPARATION TIME 15 MINUTES (PLUS REFRIGERATION TIME) **COOKING TIME** 30 MINUTES

½ cup (35g) stale breadcrumbs
1 tablespoon finely chopped
   fresh chives
2 tablespoons finely chopped
   fresh flat-leaf parsley
2 teaspoons wholegrain mustard
¼ cup (60ml) olive oil
4 porterhouse steaks (1kg)
1kg kipfler potatoes
½ cup (125ml) dry red wine
2 teaspoons cornflour
¾ cup (180ml) beef stock
2 tablespoons coarsely
   chopped fresh chives

1 Combine breadcrumbs, finely chopped chives, parsley, mustard and 2 teaspoons of the oil in small bowl.

2 Brush steaks all over with a little of the remaining oil. Divide herb mixture among steaks, pressing firmly onto one side only; refrigerate on tray, herbed-side up, for 10 minutes.

3 Preheat oven to hot.

4 Scrub unpeeled potatoes; quarter lengthways. Place potato, in single layer, in medium shallow baking dish; drizzle with 1 tablespoon of the remaining oil. Roast, uncovered, in hot oven, about 25 minutes or until browned and crisp.

5 Meanwhile, heat remaining oil in large frying pan; cook steaks, herbed-side down first, until browned both sides and cooked as desired. Remove from pan; cover to keep warm.

6 Place wine in same pan; stir until it comes to a boil. Boil 2 minutes then add blended cornflour and stock. Stir until sauce boils and thickens slightly; stir in coarsely chopped chives. Serve steaks and potatoes with sauce, accompanied by steamed green beans, if desired.

serves 4
per serving 27g fat; 2813kJ (672 cal)

rissoles with cabbage mash

PREPARATION TIME 25 MINUTES **COOKING TIME** 20 MINUTES

2 bacon rashers (140g), rind removed, chopped finely
1 small brown onion (80g), chopped finely
1 clove garlic, crushed
1 fresh red thai chilli, seeded, chopped finely
1 tablespoon worcestershire sauce
1 cup (70g) stale breadcrumbs
1 egg
¼ cup coarsely chopped fresh flat-leaf parsley
500g mince
2 tablespoons barbecue sauce
1 tablespoon vegetable oil
1 tablespoon dijon mustard
2 cups (500ml) beef stock
1 tablespoon cornflour
2 tablespoons water

CABBAGE MASH
1kg potatoes, quartered
¼ cup (60ml) cream
30g butter, chopped
200g finely shredded savoy cabbage
1 small white onion (80g), chopped finely

1 Cook potato for cabbage mash.
2 Cook bacon, onion, garlic and chilli in medium frying pan, stirring
   until onion softens. Remove from heat.
3 Using hands, combine worcestershire sauce, breadcrumbs, egg,
   parsley, mince and half of the barbecue sauce with bacon mixture in
   large bowl; shape mixture into eight rissoles.
4 Heat oil in same pan; cook rissoles, in batches, until browned both
   sides and cooked through. Cover to keep warm.
5 Place mustard, stock and remaining barbecue sauce in same pan;
   bring to a boil. Stir in blended cornflour and water; cook, stirring,
   until gravy boils and thickens slightly.
6 Finish cabbage mash. Serve rissoles, topped with gravy,
   with cabbage mash.
   CABBAGE MASH Boil, steam or microwave potato until tender;
   drain. Mash potato with cream and butter until smooth; stir in
   cabbage and onion.

serves 4
per serving 35.9g fat; 3038kJ (726 cal)
tip Rissoles can be prepared a day ahead and kept, covered,
under refrigeration.

hamburger with a twist

PREPARATION TIME 15 MINUTES **COOKING TIME** 10 MINUTES

80g gorgonzola cheese,
   crumbled

¼ cup (60g) sour cream

400g beef mince

120g sausage mince

1 small brown onion (80g),
   chopped finely

1 tablespoon barbecue sauce

2 teaspoons worcestershire
   sauce

½ cup (75g) drained sun-dried
   tomatoes in oil, chopped finely

4 hamburger buns

50g baby rocket leaves

170g marinated artichoke
   hearts, drained, quartered

1 Blend or process half of the
   cheese with the cream until
   smooth. Stir in remaining cheese.

2 Using hands, combine minces,
   onion, sauces and tomato in
   medium bowl; shape mixture
   into four hamburger patties.

3 Cook patties in large lightly oiled
   heated frying pan until browned
   both sides and cooked through.

4 Meanwhile, halve buns; toast,
   cut-side up. Sandwich rocket,
   patties, gorgonzola cream and
   artichoke in toasted buns.

serves 4
per serving 30.8g fat;
2954kJ (706 cal)

spaghetti bolognese

PREPARATION TIME 10 MINUTES **COOKING TIME** 25 MINUTES

1 tablespoon olive oil
1 medium brown onion (150g),
    chopped coarsely
2 cloves garlic, crushed
2 medium carrots (240g),
    chopped coarsely
2 trimmed celery sticks (150g),
    chopped coarsely
500g lean mince
2 x 400g cans crushed
    tomatoes
½ cup (125ml) dry red wine
⅓ cup (90g) tomato paste
1 teaspoon sugar
200g mushrooms, sliced thinly
¼ cup finely chopped
    fresh basil
375g spaghetti
¼ cup (20g) finely grated
    parmesan cheese

1 Heat oil in large saucepan; cook
   onion, garlic, carrot and celery,
   stirring, until vegetables soften.
   Add mince; cook, stirring, until
   mince is changed in colour.
   Add undrained tomatoes, wine,
   paste and sugar; cook, stirring,
   about 15 minutes or until sauce
   thickens slightly. Add mushrooms
   and basil, reduce heat; simmer,
   uncovered, 10 minutes.
2 Meanwhile, cook pasta in
   large saucepan of boiling water,
   uncovered, until just tender; drain.
3 Divide pasta among serving
   bowls; top with bolognese
   sauce, sprinkle with cheese.
   Serve with ciabatta and a
   green salad tossed with
   Italian dressing, if desired.

serves 4
per serving 17.2g fat;
2883kJ (689 cal)

twice-fried sichuan beef

PREPARATION TIME 20 MINUTES (PLUS STANDING TIME)
COOKING TIME 25 MINUTES

600g piece eye fillet, sliced thinly
2 tablespoons dry sherry
2 tablespoons salt-reduced soy sauce
1 teaspoon brown sugar
½ cup (75g) cornflour
1½ cups (300g) jasmine rice
vegetable oil, for deep-frying
2 teaspoons sesame oil
1 clove garlic, crushed
1 fresh red thai chilli, chopped finely
1 medium brown onion (150g), sliced thickly
1 medium carrot (120g), halved, sliced thinly
1 small red capsicum (150g), sliced thinly
500g gai larn, chopped coarsely
1 tablespoon cracked sichuan peppercorns
2 tablespoons oyster sauce
¼ cup (60ml) salt-reduced soy sauce, extra
½ cup (125ml) beef stock
2 teaspoons brown sugar, extra

1   Combine fillet, sherry, soy sauce and sugar in medium bowl.
    Stand 10 minutes; drain. Toss fillet in cornflour; shake off excess.
2   Meanwhile, cook rice in large saucepan of boiling water, uncovered,
    until just tender; drain. Cover to keep warm.
3   Heat vegetable oil in wok or large saucepan; deep-fry beef, in batches,
    until crisp. Drain on absorbent paper. Reserve oil for another use.
4   Heat sesame oil in same cleaned wok; stir-fry garlic, chilli and onion
    until onion softens. Add carrot and capsicum; stir-fry until just tender.
    Add gai larn; stir-fry until just wilted. Add beef with peppercorns,
    oyster sauce, extra soy sauce, stock and extra sugar; stir-fry until
    heated through. Serve beef and vegetables with rice.

serves 4
per serving 20.5g fat; 3046kJ (728 cal)
tip It is easier to slice beef thinly if it is partially frozen.

italian fennel and beef-fillet salad with balsamic vinaigrette

PREPARATION TIME 15 MINUTES (PLUS STANDING TIME) **COOKING TIME** 15 MINUTES

Scotch fillet steaks are also known as rib-eye steaks.

100g bean thread noodles
4 scotch fillet steaks (800g)
2 medium fennel bulbs (600g), sliced thinly
1 medium red onion (170g), sliced thinly
150g baby rocket leaves
1¼ cups (100g) shaved parmesan cheese

BALSAMIC VINAIGRETTE
¼ cup (60ml) lemon juice
2 cloves garlic, crushed
¼ cup (60ml) olive oil
2 tablespoons balsamic vinegar
1 tablespoon coarsely chopped fresh thyme

1 Place noodles in medium heatproof bowl; cover with boiling water, stand until just tender, drain.
2 Make balsamic vinaigrette.
3 Cook steaks on heated oiled grill plate (or grill or barbecue) until browned both sides and cooked as desired. Cover; stand 5 minutes.
4 Cut noodles into 5cm lengths; place in large bowl with fennel, onion and rocket. Slice steak thinly, add to noodles with balsamic vinaigrette; toss gently to combine. Serve salad topped with cheese.

BALSAMIC VINAIGRETTE
Combine ingredients in screw-top jar; shake well.

serves 4
per serving 34.8g fat; 2610kJ (624 cal)

beef salad with blue-cheese dressing

PREPARATION TIME 10 MINUTES (PLUS STANDING TIME) **COOKING TIME** 20 MINUTES

500g tiny new potatoes,
  quartered
1 tablespoon olive oil
4 fillet steaks (500g)
300g green beans, trimmed,
  halved crossways
200g grape tomatoes, halved
100g baby rocket leaves

BLUE-CHEESE DRESSING
¼ cup (60ml) olive oil
2 cloves garlic, crushed
¼ cup (60ml) orange juice
60g blue cheese, crumbled

1 Preheat oven to very hot.
2 Place potato, in single layer, in large shallow baking dish; drizzle with oil. Roast, uncovered, in very hot oven about 20 minutes or until lightly browned and tender.
3 Make blue-cheese dressing.
4 Cook steaks on heated oiled grill plate (or grill or barbecue) until browned both sides and cooked as desired. Cover; stand 5 minutes.
5 Meanwhile, boil, steam or microwave beans until just tender; drain.
6 Slice steak thinly. Combine steak, beans and potato in large bowl with tomato and rocket, drizzle with blue-cheese dressing; toss gently to combine.

BLUE-CHEESE DRESSING
Combine ingredients in screw-top jar; shake well.

serves 4
per serving 31.9g fat;
2143kJ (512 cal)

spaghetti and meatballs

PREPARATION TIME 20 MINUTES **COOKING TIME** 20 MINUTES

We've made twice the number of meatballs required to serve four; freeze half of the meatballs for future use, when time is short. Place half of the uncooked meatballs in a single layer on a tray, cover; freeze until solid. Remove meatballs from tray and place in either a storage container that has a tight-fitting lid, or a sealable plastic bag; return to freezer. Frozen meatballs can be thawed, then cooked directly in the pasta sauce.

1kg mince
1 small green capsicum (150g), chopped finely
1 small brown onion (80g), chopped finely
2 cloves garlic, crushed
¼ cup coarsely chopped fresh flat-leaf parsley
1 egg
1 cup (70g) stale breadcrumbs
1 teaspoon finely grated lemon rind
½ cup (130g) sun-dried tomato pesto
2 tablespoons olive oil
2 cloves garlic, crushed, extra
1 medium brown onion (150g), sliced thinly
½ cup (125ml) dry red wine
2 cups (520g) bottled tomato pasta sauce
½ cup (125ml) chicken stock
¼ cup coarsely chopped fresh basil
375g spaghetti
⅓ cup (25g) flaked parmesan cheese

1 Using hands, combine mince, capsicum, chopped onion, garlic, parsley, egg, breadcrumbs, rind and pesto in large bowl; roll level tablespoons of mince mixture into balls. Freeze half of the meatballs.
2 Heat oil in large frying pan; cook remaining meatballs, in batches, until browned all over. Drain on absorbent paper.
3 Cook extra garlic and sliced onion in same pan, stirring, until onion softens. Add wine; bring to a boil. Reduce heat; simmer, uncovered, about 5 minutes or until mixture is reduced by half. Add sauce and stock; bring to a boil.
4 Return meatballs to pan, reduce heat; simmer, uncovered, about 10 minutes or until meatballs are cooked through. Stir in basil.
5 Meanwhile, cook pasta in large saucepan of boiling water, uncovered, until just tender; drain.
6 Divide pasta among serving bowls; top with meatballs and sauce, serve with cheese.

serves 4
per serving 30.7g fat; 3442kJ (822 cal)

beef kway teow

PREPARATION TIME 10 MINUTES **COOKING TIME** 15 MINUTES

So popular in Singapore and throughout the Malay peninsula that they're practically regarded as fast food, kway teow are fresh, flat, wide rice noodles fried with meat or seafood and assorted vegetables. Beef strips can be prepared from blade, fillet, rib-eye, round, rump, sirloin or topside steak.

2 tablespoons peanut oil
500g beef strips
450g fresh wide rice noodles
3 cloves garlic, crushed
2 teaspoons grated fresh ginger
6 green onions, cut into
  2cm pieces
1 small red capsicum (150g),
  sliced thinly
2 cups (160g) bean sprouts
¼ cup (75g) satay sauce
2 tablespoons fish sauce

1 Heat half of the oil in wok or large frying pan; stir-fry beef, in batches, until browned all over.
2 Place noodles in large heatproof bowl; cover with boiling water, separate with fork, drain.
3 Heat remaining oil in wok; stir-fry garlic and ginger until fragrant. Add onion and capsicum; stir-fry until vegetables are just soft. Return beef to wok with noodles, sprouts and sauces; stir-fry until heated through.

serves 4
per serving 22g fat; 1913kJ (457 cal)

stir-fried beef, bok choy and gai larn

PREPARATION TIME 10 MINUTES **COOKING TIME** 25 MINUTES

Beef strips can be prepared from blade, fillet, rib-eye, round, rump, sirloin or topside steak.

1½ cups (300g) jasmine rice
2 tablespoons peanut oil
500g beef strips
2 cloves garlic, crushed
2 teaspoons grated fresh ginger
1 tablespoon finely chopped
    fresh lemon grass
2 fresh red thai chillies,
    seeded, sliced thinly
1kg baby bok choy,
    chopped coarsely
500g gai larn, chopped coarsely
4 green onions, sliced thinly
2 tablespoons kecap manis
1 tablespoon fish sauce
¼ cup (60ml) sweet chilli sauce
¼ cup coarsely chopped
    fresh coriander

1 Cook rice in large saucepan of boiling water, uncovered, until just tender; drain. Cover to keep warm.
2 Meanwhile, heat half of the oil in wok or large frying pan; stir-fry beef, in batches, until browned all over.
3 Heat remaining oil in same wok; stir-fry garlic, ginger, lemon grass and chilli until fragrant. Add vegetables; stir-fry until vegetables just wilt. Return beef to wok with remaining ingredients; stir-fry until heated through. Serve with rice.

serves 4
per serving 18.4g fat;
2481kJ (593 cal)

corned beef hash with fried eggs

PREPARATION TIME 30 MINUTES (PLUS COOLING TIME)
COOKING TIME 20 MINUTES

If you have enough leftover meat from our traditional corned beef recipe (see page 48), it can be used here. Keep in mind, however, that the other ingredients must be used in the same proportion to the meat as in the recipe below.

500g piece cooked corned beef
3 medium potatoes (600g), quartered
1 medium carrot (120g), grated coarsely
4 green onions, chopped coarsely
2 eggs, beaten lightly
2 tablespoons plain flour
¼ cup (60ml) olive oil
4 eggs, extra
½ long loaf pide

1 Use two forks to shred corned beef finely.
2 Meanwhile, boil, steam or microwave potato until just tender; drain. Cool 10 minutes; grate coarsely. Using hands, combine potato with corned beef in large bowl; add carrot, onion, egg and flour, shape mixture into eight patties.
3 Heat half of the oil in large frying pan; cook patties, in batches, until browned both sides and crisp. Cover to keep warm.
4 Heat remaining oil in same pan; cook extra eggs, uncovered, until eggs are cooked as desired.
5 Meanwhile, cut bread in half then split each piece in half horizontally; toast, cut-side up. Place one toast piece on each serving plate; top with two patties and one egg. Serve with tomato sauce, if desired.

serves 4
per serving 31g fat; 2975kJ (711 cal)

venetian calves liver and onions

PREPARATION TIME 10 MINUTES **COOKING TIME** 25 MINUTES

A traditional Venetian dish, the classic fegato alla veneziana is found on the menus of Italian restaurants around the world yet is easy enough to make at home. The secret to its success is that the calves liver should be sliced into paper-thin scallops then quickly seared – overcooking will toughen its delicate texture.

2 cups (500ml) water
2 cups (500ml) milk
1 cup (170g) polenta
½ cup (40g) finely grated parmesan cheese
½ cup (125ml) cream
¼ cup coarsely chopped fresh flat-leaf parsley
40g butter
2 tablespoons olive oil
3 medium brown onions (450g), sliced thinly
2 teaspoons cornflour
¾ cup (180ml) beef stock
2 teaspoons dijon mustard
500g calves liver, sliced thinly
½ teaspoon balsamic vinegar

1 Combine the water and milk in large saucepan; bring to a boil. Add polenta in a slow, steady stream, stirring constantlly. Reduce heat; simmer, stirring occasionally, about 20 minutes or until polenta thickens. Stir in cheese, cream and parsley. Cover to keep warm.
2 Meanwhile, heat butter and half of the oil in large frying pan; cook onion, stirring, until onion softens. Stir in blended cornflour, stock and mustard; cook, stirring, until sauce boils and thickens.
3 Heat remaining oil in large frying pan; cook liver quickly over high heat until browned both sides and cooked as desired.
4 Stir vinegar into sauce just before serving with polenta and liver; accompany with a balsamic-dressed mixed green salad, if desired.

serves 4
per serving 47.2g fat; 3171kJ (757 cal)

breaded veal cutlets with gnocchi in garlic mushroom sauce

PREPARATION TIME 15 MINUTES (PLUS REFRIGERATION TIME) **COOKING TIME** 35 MINUTES

2 eggs, beaten lightly
2 tablespoons milk
¼ cup (35g) plain flour
¾ cup (75g) packaged breadcrumbs
¾ cup (50g) stale breadcrumbs
¾ cup (80g) pizza cheese
½ cup coarsely chopped fresh flat-leaf parsley
8 veal cutlets (1kg)
¼ cup (60ml) olive oil
2 cloves garlic, sliced thinly
250g mushrooms, sliced thinly
¾ cup (180ml) cream
½ cup (125ml) beef stock
625g packaged potato gnocchi

1 Whisk egg, milk and flour in medium bowl. Combine crumbs, cheese and ⅓ cup of the parsley in another medium bowl. Coat cutlets, one at a time, in egg mixture then in cheese mixture. Place cutlets, in single layer, on tray. Cover; refrigerate 10 minutes.

2 Heat half of the oil in large frying pan; cook cutlets, in batches, until browned both sides and cooked as desired. Cover to keep warm.

3 Heat remaining oil in same pan; cook garlic and mushrooms, stirring, until mushrooms are just tender. Add cream and stock; bring to a boil. Reduce heat; simmer, stirring, until sauce thickens slightly.

4 Meanwhile, cook gnocchi in large saucepan of boiling water, uncovered, until gnocchi float to the surface. Remove from pan with slotted spoon; place in large bowl.

5 Stir remaining parsley into sauce; pour sauce over gnocchi, toss to combine. Serve gnocchi with cutlets and, if desired, steamed green beans.

serves 4
per serving 46.8g fat; 4206kJ (1005 cal)

new york steaks with lemon thyme butter

PREPARATION TIME 15 MINUTES (PLUS REFRIGERATION TIME) **COOKING TIME** 45 MINUTES

New York-cut steaks are also known as boneless sirloin steaks.

4 large potatoes (1.2kg),
    cut into wedges
2 medium red onions (340g),
    cut into wedges
1 medium lemon (140g),
    cut into wedges
2 teaspoons fresh thyme leaves
¼ cup (60ml) olive oil
4 new york-cut steaks (880g)

LEMON THYME BUTTER
60g butter, softened
2 teaspoons finely grated
    lemon rind
1 teaspoon finely chopped
    fresh thyme
1 clove garlic, crushed

1 Preheat oven to hot. Make lemon thyme butter.
2 Combine potato, onion, lemon, thyme and oil in large deep baking dish. Roast, uncovered, in hot oven, stirring occasionally, about 45 minutes or until potato is browned and crisp.
3 Meanwhile, cook steaks, in batches, on heated oiled grill plate (or grill or barbecue) until browned both sides and cooked as desired.
4 Serve steaks with potato and onion mixture topped with lemon thyme butter.
   LEMON THYME BUTTER
   Combine ingredients in small bowl. Cover; refrigerate until firm.

serves 4
per serving 47g fat;
3434kJ (820 cal)

reuben salad

PREPARATION TIME 15 MINUTES **COOKING TIME** 10 MINUTES

The inspiration for this tasty salad is that famous New York deli sandwich, the Reuben, a universal favourite ever since its creation in the early 1900s. Sliced leftover meat from our traditional corned beef recipe (see page 48) can be used in this recipe.

4 medium potatoes (800g),
   cut into 2cm cubes
2 tablespoons mayonnaise
1 tablespoon mild chilli sauce
1 teaspoon horseradish cream
2 green onions, chopped finely
400g can sauerkraut, drained
1 tablespoon finely chopped
   fresh chives
4 slices rye bread
12 slices corned beef (360g)
180g swiss cheese, sliced thinly
4 large dill pickles (260g)

1 Boil, steam or microwave potato until just tender; drain. Cool, 5 minutes.

2 Combine potato in medium bowl with combined mayonnaise, chilli sauce, horseradish cream and onion. Combine sauerkraut and chives in small bowl.

3 Divide bread, corned beef, cheese, potato mixture and sliced pickles among serving plates; serve with sauerkraut mixture.

serves 4
per serving 23.6g fat;
2368kJ (566 cal)

saltimbocca with risotto milanese

PREPARATION TIME 10 MINUTES **COOKING TIME** 25 MINUTES

Saltimbocca is a classic Italian veal dish that literally means "jump in the mouth" – just the sensation the wonderful flavours will produce with your first bite. Tinged with the taste and colour of saffron, a Milanese is the classic risotto generally served with saltimbocca.

8 veal steaks (680g)
4 slices prosciutto (60g), halved crossways
8 fresh sage leaves
½ cup (50g) finely grated pecorino cheese
40g butter
1 cup (250ml) dry white wine
1 tablespoon coarsely chopped fresh sage
RISOTTO MILANESE
1½ cups (375ml) water
2 cups (500ml) chicken stock
½ cup (125ml) dry white wine
¼ teaspoon saffron threads
20g butter
1 large brown onion (200g), chopped finely
2 cups (400g) arborio rice
¼ cup (20g) finely grated parmesan cheese

1 Place steaks on board. Place one piece prosciutto, one sage leaf and ⅛ of the cheese on each steak; fold in half to secure filling, secure with a toothpick or small skewer.
2 Make risotto milanese.
3 Melt half of the butter in medium non-stick frying pan; cook saltimbocca, in batches, about 5 minutes or until browned both sides and cooked through. Cover to keep warm.
4 Pour wine into same frying pan; bring to a boil. Boil, uncovered, until wine reduces by half. Stir in remaining butter then chopped sage.
5 Divide risotto milanese and saltimbocca among serving plates; drizzle saltimbocca with sauce and accompany with steamed green beans, if desired.
RISOTTO MILANESE Place the water, stock, wine and saffron in medium saucepan; bring to a boil. Reduce heat; simmer, covered. Heat butter in another medium saucepan; cook onion, stirring, until softened. Add rice; stir to coat rice in onion mixture. Stir in ½ cup of the simmering stock mixture; cook, stirring, over low heat, until liquid is absorbed. Continue adding stock mixture, in ½-cup batches, stirring until absorbed after each addition. Total cooking time should be about 35 minutes or until rice is just tender. Stir cheese gently into risotto.

serves 4
per serving 23.3g fat; 3429kJ (819 cal)

moroccan beef with citrus couscous

PREPARATION TIME 15 MINUTES (PLUS STANDING TIME) **COOKING TIME** 20 MINUTES

Harissa is a paste made from dried red chillies, garlic, oil and caraway seeds, and is a staple of Moroccan cooking. Preserved lemons, a prominent ingredient in North African cooking, are lemons which have been bottled in salt and oil for several months; their flavour is subtle and perfumed. Rinse the lemons well then remove and discard flesh, using the rind only. Butt fillet is fillet from the rump; rump steak can be substituted here.

2 cloves garlic, crushed
1 teaspoon ground ginger
1 tablespoon ground cumin
2 teaspoons ground coriander
500g piece butt fillet
1 tablespoon harissa
1 cup (250ml) beef stock
200g seeded green olives, crushed slightly
½ cup coarsely chopped fresh coriander

CITRUS COUSCOUS
2 medium oranges (480g)
1 cup (250ml) water
1 cup (250ml) orange juice
2 cups (400g) couscous
¼ cup (35g) toasted slivered almonds
1 tablespoon thinly sliced preserved lemon
1 small red onion (100g), sliced thinly
500g red radishes, trimmed, sliced thinly

1 Combine garlic and spices in medium bowl; reserve about a third of the spice mixture. Add fillet to bowl with remaining two-thirds of the spice mixture; toss to coat fillet all over. Cook fillet on heated oiled grill plate (or grill or barbecue) until charred lightly both sides and cooked as desired. Cover; stand 10 minutes.

2 Make citrus couscous.

3 Meanwhile, cook harissa and remaining spice mixture in dry heated small non-stick frying pan until fragrant. Add stock; bring to a boil. Reduce heat; simmer, uncovered, about 3 minutes or until harissa dressing reduces by half. Remove from heat; stir in olives and coriander. Serve sliced fillet on citrus couscous, drizzle with warm harissa dressing.

CITRUS COUSCOUS Remove skin and white pith from oranges; cut in half, slice thinly. Place the water and juice in medium saucepan; bring to a boil. Remove from heat; stir in couscous. Cover; stand about 5 minutes or until liquid is absorbed, fluffing with fork occasionally. Add orange and remaining ingredients; toss gently to combine.

serves 4
per serving 15.5g fat; 3114kJ (744 cal)

steaks with parsnip potato mash

PREPARATION TIME 10 MINUTES (PLUS MARINATING TIME) **COOKING TIME** 20 MINUTES

New York-cut steaks are also known as boneless sirloin steaks.

4 new york-cut steaks (880g)
½ cup (125ml) plum sauce
⅓ cup (80ml) tomato sauce
⅓ cup (80ml) worcestershire
   sauce
2 cloves garlic, crushed
2 green onions, chopped finely
1kg potatoes,
   chopped coarsely
2 medium parsnips (250g),
   chopped coarsely
40g butter, chopped
⅓ cup (80ml) cream
250g baby spinach leaves

1 Combine steaks in large bowl with sauces, garlic and onion; toss to coat steaks all over in marinade. Cover; refrigerate 30 minutes.
2 Meanwhile, boil, steam or microwave potato and parsnip together until just tender; drain. Mash with butter and cream in large bowl until smooth. Cover to keep warm.
3 Drain steaks; discard marinade. Cook steaks on heated oiled grill plate (or grill or barbecue) until browned both sides and cooked as desired.
4 Boil, steam or microwave spinach until just wilted; drain. Serve steaks with parsnip potato mash and spinach.

serves 4
per serving 37.7g fat;
3475kJ (830 cal)

fettuccine with creamy tomato sausage sauce

PREPARATION TIME 10 MINUTES **COOKING TIME** 30 MINUTES

cooking-oil spray
6 thick italian sausages (480g)
2 cloves garlic, crushed
400g can crushed tomatoes
¼ cup (60ml) dry white wine
300ml cream
375g fettuccine
6 green onions, chopped finely
2 tablespoons fresh
  sage leaves

1 Lightly spray large frying pan with oil; cook sausages until browned all over and cooked through. Remove sausages from pan; chop coarsely. Cover to keep warm. Drain excess oil from pan.

2 Combine garlic, undrained tomatoes, wine and cream in same pan; bring to a boil. Reduce heat; simmer, uncovered, about 10 minutes or until sauce thickens slightly.

3 Meanwhile, cook pasta in large saucepan of boiling water, uncovered, until just tender; drain. Divide among serving bowls.

4 Stir sausage with onion and sage into tomato mixture; spoon sauce over pasta.

serves 4
per serving 64.5g fat;
4182kJ (999 cal)

thai char-grilled beef salad

PREPARATION TIME 20 MINUTES (PLUS REFRIGERATION AND STANDING TIME)
COOKING TIME 5 MINUTES

This is a loose interpretation of one of our favourite Thai dishes, yum nuah, and is a good introduction to the flavours of South-East Asian cuisine. Rib-eye, boneless sirloin or eye fillet steaks are all good substitutes for rump in this recipe.

600g piece rump steak
2 teaspoons sesame oil
⅓ cup (80ml) kecap manis
1 cup loosely packed fresh mint leaves
1 cup loosely packed fresh coriander leaves
½ cup loosely packed fresh thai basil leaves
6 green onions, sliced thinly
5 shallots (60g), sliced thinly
250g cherry tomatoes, halved
1 telegraph cucumber (400g), seeded, sliced thinly
10 kaffir lime leaves, shredded finely
100g mesclun
SWEET AND SOUR DRESSING
½ cup (125ml) lime juice
¼ cup (60ml) fish sauce
2 teaspoons sugar
2 fresh red thai chillies, sliced thinly

1 Place steak in shallow dish; brush all over with combined oil and kecap manis. Cover; refrigerate 30 minutes.
2 Meanwhile, combine herbs, onion, shallot, tomato and cucumber in large bowl; toss gently to combine.
3 Make sweet and sour dressing.
4 Cook steak on heated oiled grill plate (or grill or barbecue) until charred lightly and cooked as desired. Stand, covered, 10 minutes; slice thinly.
5 Place steak, lime leaves and mesclun in bowl with herb mixture. Add sweet and sour dressing; toss gently to combine.
SWEET AND SOUR DRESSING Combine ingredients in screw-top jar; shake well.

serves 4
per serving 12.8g fat; 1275kJ (305 cal)
tip Thai basil, also known as horapa, has a sweet licorice flavour; it is one of the basic flavours that typify Thai cuisine.

veal steaks with italian white bean salad

PREPARATION TIME 15 MINUTES **COOKING TIME** 10 MINUTES

Many varieties of already cooked white beans are available canned, among them cannellini, butter and haricot; any of these are suitable here.

1 tablespoon olive oil
8 veal steaks (680g)
½ cup (125ml) beef stock
60g butter
ITALIAN WHITE BEAN SALAD
100g baby rocket leaves
1 large tomato (250g), chopped coarsely
½ cup firmly packed fresh basil leaves, torn
2 x 400g cans white beans, rinsed, drained
1 tablespoon finely chopped fresh chives
¼ cup (60ml) lemon juice
2 cloves garlic, crushed
¼ cup (60ml) olive oil

1 Make the Italian white bean salad.
2 Heat oil in large non-stick frying pan; cook steaks, in batches, until browned both sides and cooked as desired. Cover to keep warm.
3 Pour stock into same pan; bring to a boil, stirring. Add butter, stir until butter melts. Reduce heat; simmer, stirring, 2 minutes.
4 Serve steak, drizzled with sauce, with Italian white bean salad.
ITALIAN WHITE BEAN SALAD Combine rocket, tomato, basil and beans in large bowl. Combine chives, juice, garlic and oil in screw-top jar; shake well. Pour dressing over salad; toss gently to combine.

serves 4
per serving 36.6g fat; 2450kJ (585 cal)

veal cutlets with couscous salad

PREPARATION TIME 10 MINUTES (PLUS MARINATING TIME) **COOKING TIME** 10 MINUTES

8 veal cutlets (1kg)
⅓ cup (80ml) balsamic vinegar
⅓ cup (80ml) olive oil
1 clove garlic, crushed
1½ cups (375ml) beef stock
1½ cups (300g) couscous
150g fetta cheese, cut into
  2cm pieces
⅔ cup (100g) seeded
  kalamata olives
1 medium red capsicum (200g),
  chopped coarsely
¼ cup coarsely chopped
  fresh mint
¼ cup (60ml) lemon juice
⅓ cup (80ml) olive oil, extra
1 clove garlic, crushed

1 Combine cutlets in large bowl
   with vinegar, oil and garlic;
   toss to coat cutlets all over in
   marinade. Cover; refrigerate
   20 minutes.
2 Meanwhile, bring stock to a boil
   in medium saucepan. Remove
   from heat; stir in couscous.
   Cover; stand about 5 minutes
   or until liquid is absorbed,
   fluffing with fork occasionally.
   Add remaining ingredients;
   toss gently to combine.
3 Drain cutlets; discard marinade.
   Cook cutlets on heated oiled
   grill plate (or grill or barbecue)
   until browned both sides and
   cooked as desired. Serve
   couscous salad with cutlets.

serves 4
per serving 50.8g fat;
4094kJ (978 cal)

chilli T-bones with hash browns

PREPARATION TIME 15 MINUTES (PLUS MARINATING TIME) **COOKING TIME** 20 MINUTES

4 T-bone steaks (1.2kg)
⅓ cup (80ml) worcestershire sauce
⅓ cup (80ml) hot chilli sauce
3 medium potatoes (600g)
40g butter
1 small brown onion (80g),
   chopped finely
1 bacon rasher (75g),
   chopped finely

1 Combine steaks and sauces in
   large bowl; toss to coat steaks
   all over in marinade. Cover;
   refrigerate 20 minutes.
2 Meanwhile, grate peeled potatoes
   coarsely. Using hands, squeeze
   excess liquid from potato; spread
   onto sheets of absorbent paper,
   squeeze again to remove as much
   liquid as possible from potato.
3 Heat half of the butter in large
   non-stick frying pan; cook onion
   and bacon, stirring, until onion
   softens. Add potato; stir over heat
   constantly until potato begins to
   stick to pan. Remove from heat;
   cool 5 minutes. Transfer potato
   mixture to large bowl.
4 Using wet hands, shape potato
   mixture into eight patties. Heat
   remaining butter in same pan;
   cook hash browns, in batches,
   until browned and crisp both sides.
   Drain on absorbent paper.
5 Drain steaks; discard marinade.
   Cook steaks, in batches, on heated
   oiled grill plate (or grill or barbecue)
   until browned both sides and
   cooked as desired. Serve steaks
   with hash browns, accompanied
   by barbecued corn cobs and a
   sliced tomato salad, if desired.

serves 4
per serving 22.8g fat;
2155kJ (515 cal)

mustard-crusted rack of veal with kumara mash

PREPARATION TIME 25 MINUTES **COOKING TIME** 35 MINUTES

2 tablespoons wholegrain mustard
3 green onions, chopped finely
2 cloves garlic, crushed
1 tablespoon finely chopped fresh rosemary
2 tablespoons olive oil
1kg veal rack (8 cutlets), trimmed
2 small kumara (500g), chopped coarsely
20g butter
⅓ cup (80ml) cream
1 large brown onion (200g), sliced thinly
400g mushrooms, sliced thinly
1 tablespoon plain flour
¼ cup (60ml) dry white wine
¾ cup (180ml) chicken stock
¼ cup coarsely chopped fresh flat-leaf parsley

1   Preheat oven to moderately hot.
2   Combine mustard, green onion, half of the garlic, rosemary and
     half of the oil in small jug. Place veal on wire rack over large shallow
     flameproof baking dish; coat veal all over with mustard mixture.
     Roast, uncovered, in moderately hot oven, about 30 minutes or until
     browned all over and cooked as desired. Cover to keep warm.
3   Meanwhile, boil, steam or microwave kumara until tender; drain. Mash
     kumara in large bowl with butter and half of the cream until smooth.
4   Heat remaining oil in same flameproof dish; cook brown onion
     and remaining garlic, stirring, until onion softens. Add mushrooms;
     cook, stirring, about 5 minutes or until just tender. Add flour; cook,
     stirring, until mixture thickens and bubbles. Gradually stir in wine
     and stock; stir until sauce boils and thickens. Add remaining cream
     and parsley; stir until heated through.
5   Serve veal with kumara mash and mushroom sauce.

serves 4
per serving   26.2g fat; 2302kJ (550 cal)

mee goreng

PREPARATION TIME 10 MINUTES **COOKING TIME** 15 MINUTES

Mee goreng, from Indonesia and Malaysia, simply translates
as fried noodles and is an everyday dish in that part of the world.
Beef strips can be prepared from blade, fillet, rib-eye, round, rump,
sirloin or topside steak.

600g hokkien noodles
1 tablespoon peanut oil
3 eggs, beaten lightly
500g beef strips
2 cloves garlic, crushed
2 teaspoons grated fresh ginger
500g baby bok choy, chopped coarsely
4 green onions, sliced thinly
¼ cup coarsely chopped fresh coriander
2 tablespoons dried shrimp
¼ cup (60ml) kecap manis
2 teaspoons sambal oelek
¼ cup (60ml) beef stock
½ cup (75g) roasted unsalted peanuts, chopped coarsely

1 Place noodles in large heatproof bowl; cover with boiling water,
   separate with fork, drain.
2 Heat a quarter of the oil in wok or large frying pan; cook half of the
   egg, over medium heat, tilting pan, until egg mixture is almost set.
   Remove omelette from wok; repeat with another quarter of the oil
   and remaining egg. Roll omelettes tightly; slice thinly.
3 Heat remaining oil in same wok; stir-fry combined beef, garlic and ginger,
   in batches, until beef is browned all over and just cooked through.
   Place bok choy in same wok; stir-fry until just wilted. Return beef to
   pan with noodles, onion, coriander, shrimp and combined kecap manis,
   sambal and stock; stir-fry until heated through. Serve mee goreng
   topped with omelette and peanuts.

serves 4
per serving 27.5g fat; 2547kJ (608 cal)

steak and chips

PREPARATION TIME 10 MINUTES (PLUS STANDING TIME) **COOKING TIME** 30 MINUTES

Bring Paris into your kitchen with this classic French bistro version of steak and chips ("bifteck frites"): a tender piece of beef, grilled to perfection, served with freshly made skinny fries and a generous dollop of mustard cream sauce. We used beef fillet from the rump (also called butt fillet), but rib-eye, boneless sirloin or eye fillet steaks are all suitable. Sebago or bintje potatoes are best suited to this recipe.

1kg potatoes
vegetable oil, for deep-frying
1 tablespoon olive oil
1kg piece butt fillet,
    cut into 4 steaks
¾ cup (180ml) dry white wine
250g crème fraîche
1 tablespoon wholegrain
    mustard

1   Cut potatoes into 5mm slices, then each slice into thin 5mm chips. Place chips in large bowl of cold water; stand 30 minutes. Drain; pat chips dry with absorbent paper.
2   Heat vegetable oil in large saucepan; deep-fry chips, in batches, about 5 minutes or until browned lightly. Drain chips on absorbent paper; cover to keep warm.
3   Meanwhile, heat olive oil in large frying pan; cook steaks, in batches, until browned both sides and cooked as desired. Cover to keep warm.
4   Place wine in same frying pan; bring to a boil, stirring. Reduce heat; simmer, uncovered, 1 minute. Whisk in crème fraîche and mustard; simmer, uncovered, about 2 minutes or until sauce thickens slightly. Serve sauce with steak and chips.

serves 4
per serving 60.5g fat;
4055kJ (969 cal)

easy wonton lasagne stacks

PREPARATION TIME 20 MINUTES **COOKING TIME** 1 HOUR

600g mince
2 tablespoons tomato paste
2 green onions, chopped finely
2 eggs, beaten lightly
250g ricotta
2 tablespoons finely shredded
  fresh basil
12 wonton wrappers
½ cup (55g) pizza cheese
700g bottled tomato
  pasta sauce

1 Preheat oven to moderate.
2 Using hands, combine mince, paste, onion and half of the egg in medium bowl; roll mince mixture into eight patties.
3 Combine ricotta, basil and remaining egg in separate medium bowl.
4 Place four wrappers, in single layer, in shallow 2-litre (8 cup) square baking dish; top each wrapper with one patty. Divide half of the ricotta mixture among patties; sprinkle with half of the pizza cheese. Top each stack with one of the remaining wrappers; repeat layering with remaining patties, ricotta mixture and cheese, finishing with remaining wrappers.
5 Pour sauce over lasagne stacks; cook, uncovered, in moderate oven, about 50 minutes or until stacks are cooked through and set. Serve with crusty Italian bread and a mixed green salad dressed in a white wine vinaigrette, if desired.

serves 4
per serving 29.3g fat;
2231kJ (533 cal)

weekends

On weekends, when there's more time to cook, it's fun to entertain friends or treat your family with something special. These recipes take somewhat longer to cook but they're uncomplicated, easy to prepare... and so mouth-wateringly special that everyone at the table will hope the weekend never ends.

roasted eye fillet with red wine risotto

PREPARATION TIME 15 MINUTES **COOKING TIME** 40 MINUTES (PLUS STANDING TIME)

500g piece eye fillet
1 tablespoon olive oil
1 teaspoon ground black pepper
¼ cup (60ml) dry red wine
½ cup (125ml) beef stock

RED WINE RISOTTO

3 cups (750ml) vegetable stock
40g butter
1 medium brown onion (150g),
  chopped finely
1 cup (200g) arborio rice
1 cup (250ml) dry red wine
¼ cup (20g) finely grated
  parmesan cheese
3 green onions, sliced thinly

1 Preheat oven to moderately hot.
2 Trim excess fat from fillet; tie fillet with kitchen string at 3cm intervals. Place fillet in lightly oiled shallow flameproof baking dish; brush all over with oil, sprinkle with pepper. Roast, uncovered, in moderately hot oven, about 20 minutes or until cooked as desired.
3 Meanwhile, start making red wine risotto.
4 Remove fillet from dish, cover; stand 10 minutes. Place baking dish over low heat, add wine; simmer, stirring, about 2 minutes or until mixture reduces by half. Add stock; stir until sauce comes to a boil. Strain sauce into small jug. Serve sliced fillet with red wine risotto, drizzled with sauce.

RED WINE RISOTTO Place stock in medium saucepan; bring to a boil. Reduce heat; simmer, covered. Heat half of the butter in large saucepan; cook brown onion, stirring, until softened. Add rice; stir to coat rice in onion mixture. Add wine; bring to a boil. Reduce heat; simmer, stirring, 2 minutes. Stir in ½ cup of the simmering stock; cook, stirring, over low heat, until liquid is absorbed. Continue adding stock mixture, in ½-cup batches, stirring until absorbed after each addition. Total cooking time should be about 35 minutes or until rice is just tender. Add cheese, remaining butter and green onion, stirring until butter melts.

serves 4
per serving 23.2g fat; 2397kJ (573 cal)
tip This risotto is quite thick and creamy; if this is not to your taste, stir in a little boiling water just before serving.

beef roulade

PREPARATION TIME 20 MINUTES (PLUS REFRIGERATION TIME) **COOKING TIME** 55 MINUTES

500g lean mince
1 small brown onion (80g), chopped finely
2 cloves garlic, crushed
1 egg
1 tablespoon tomato paste
1 tablespoon coarsely chopped fresh basil
2 cups (140g) stale breadcrumbs
40g baby spinach leaves
6 slices prosciutto (90g)
9 cherry tomatoes (150g)
TOMATO AND MUSTARD SAUCE
½ cup (125ml) tomato sauce
2 tablespoons barbecue sauce
2 tablespoons dijon mustard
¼ cup (60ml) water

1 Grease 25cm x 30cm swiss roll pan; line with baking paper, extending paper 5cm over the edge of both long sides.
2 Using hands, combine mince, onion, garlic, egg, paste, basil and breadcrumbs in large bowl; press mixture into prepared pan, top with spinach leaves then prosciutto.
3 Place cherry tomatoes along one long side. Starting with this side, lift paper and roll, holding filling in place as you roll away from you, pressing roll gently but tightly around filling. Discard paper, wrap roll in foil; refrigerate 20 minutes. Preheat oven to hot.
4 Make tomato and mustard sauce.
5 Place roulade, still wrapped in foil, on oven tray; bake in hot oven 40 minutes. Unwrap roulade; bake on oven tray in hot oven about 15 minutes or until browned. Serve roulade, sliced, with tomato and mustard sauce, and accompanied by creamy polenta, if desired.
TOMATO AND MUSTARD SAUCE Combine ingredients in small saucepan; cook, stirring, until heated through.

serves 4
per serving 13g fat; 1804kJ (431 cal)

traditional corned beef with horseradish white sauce

PREPARATION TIME 20 MINUTES **COOKING TIME** 2 HOURS 20 MINUTES

1.5 litres (6 cups) water
1.5kg piece silverside
4 cloves
1 medium brown onion (150g),
    chopped coarsely
2 trimmed sticks celery (150g),
    chopped coarsely
2 cloves garlic, peeled
2 x 4cm strips orange rind
2 cups (500ml) beef stock
500g tiny new potatoes,
    quartered
2 medium green zucchini (240g),
    sliced thickly
250g green beans, trimmed
2 teaspoons olive oil
2 green onions, chopped finely
¼ cup (60ml) dry white wine
¾ cup (180ml) cream
2 teaspoons horseradish cream
¼ cup coarsely chopped
    fresh flat-leaf parsley

1 Combine the water, silverside, cloves, brown onion, celery, garlic, rind and stock in large saucepan; bring to a boil. Reduce heat; simmer, covered, 2 hours.

2 Reserving cooking liquid, drain corned beef; wrap in foil to keep warm. Strain liquid into large saucepan; discard solids. Return liquid to a boil; add potato. Reduce heat; simmer, uncovered, about 5 minutes or until just tender. Add zucchini and beans; cook, uncovered, until vegetables are just tender. Drain; discard cooking liquid.

3 Meanwhile, heat oil in medium frying pan; cook green onion, stirring, until just tender. Add wine; bring to a boil. Boil, uncovered, until mixture reduces by half. Add cream and horseradish cream; cook, stirring, about 3 minutes or until sauce thickens slightly. Stir in parsley.

4 Slice corned beef thinly. Place slices with vegetables on serving plates; pour sauce over corned beef.

serves 4
per serving 38.8g fat; 2994kJ (715 cal)
tip Any leftover corned beef can be used in the recipes for corned beef hash (see page 18) or reuben salad (see page 25).

veal rack with rosemary and rocket pesto

PREPARATION TIME 15 MINUTES **COOKING TIME** 1 HOUR 5 MINUTES (PLUS STANDING TIME)

1kg tiny new potatoes
1 clove garlic, quartered
50g baby rocket leaves
¼ cup (60ml) extra virgin olive oil
¼ cup coarsely chopped fresh rosemary
1kg veal rack (8 cutlets)
½ cup (40g) finely grated parmesan cheese
1 tablespoon plain flour
¾ cup (180ml) beef stock
¼ cup (60ml) dry white wine
1 tablespoon redcurrant jelly
500g asparagus, trimmed

1 Preheat oven to moderately hot.
2 Place potatoes in lightly oiled shallow medium baking dish; roast, uncovered, in moderately hot oven about 50 minutes or until tender.
3 Meanwhile, blend or process garlic, rocket, oil and 2 tablespoons of the rosemary until mixture forms a paste. Stir remaining rosemary into pesto.
4 Place veal rack on wire rack over large shallow flameproof baking dish; coat veal with pesto. Roast, uncovered, in moderately hot oven about 40 minutes or until veal is browned and cooked as desired. Remove veal from dish; cover to keep warm.
5 When potatoes are tender, sprinkle with cheese; roast, uncovered, about 5 minutes or until cheese melts.
6 Place flameproof baking dish holding veal juices over heat, add flour; cook, stirring, until mixture thickens and bubbles. Gradually add stock, wine and jelly, stirring, until sauce boils and thickens slightly.
7 Meanwhile, boil, steam or microwave asparagus until just tender; drain.
8 Serve veal, sliced into cutlets, with potatoes, asparagus and sauce.

serves 4
per serving 21g fat; 2487kJ (594 cal)

veal braciole with rice and peas

PREPARATION TIME 25 MINUTES **COOKING TIME** 40 MINUTES

The Italian veal cut known as braciole is similar to a schnitzel or scallop, a thinly sliced piece cut from the leg and fairly free of fat. In some parts of Italy, when a braciole is filled and rolled, it is known as an involtino. Whatever name it goes under, it must be browned quickly to avoid excessive shrinkage and toughness. Italian rice and peas ("risi e bisi") is a classic Venetian dish – try making it with fresh baby peas.

8 slices pancetta (120g)
8 veal schnitzels (800g)
⅔ cup (100g) drained sun-dried tomatoes in oil, sliced thinly
⅓ cup (55g) seeded green olives, sliced thinly
1 tablespoon drained baby capers, rinsed
2 teaspoons fresh marjoram leaves
1 tablespoon olive oil
RICE AND PEAS
1 litre (4 cups) water
2 cups (500ml) chicken stock
40g butter
2 cups (400g) arborio rice
1 cup (125g) frozen baby peas
1 cup (80g) finely grated parmesan cheese
¼ cup finely chopped fresh flat-leaf parsley

1 Preheat oven to moderate.
2 Place one slice of pancetta on each schnitzel; divide tomato, olives, capers and marjoram between schnitzels.
3 Roll schnitzels to enclose filling; tie with kitchen string to secure.
4 Start making rice and peas.
5 Heat oil in large frying pan; cook braciole, uncovered, until browned all over. Place on oven tray; bake, uncovered, in moderate oven about 10 minutes or until cooked through.
6 Serve braciole with rice and peas.
RICE AND PEAS Place the water and stock in medium saucepan; bring to a boil. Reduce heat; simmer, covered. Melt butter in large saucepan, add rice; stir until rice is coated in butter and slightly opaque. Stir in 1 cup of the hot stock mixture; cook, stirring, over low heat, until liquid is absorbed. Continue adding stock mixture, in 1-cup batches, stirring until absorbed after each addition. Add peas with last cup of stock mixture; stir in cheese and parsley.

serves 4
per serving 30.4g fat; 3938kJ (941 cal)

steak sandwich revisited

PREPARATION TIME 20 MINUTES **COOKING TIME** I HOUR 20 MINUTES

Scotch fillet steak is also known as rib-eye steak. We used a loaf
of ciabatta for this recipe.

4 scotch fillet steaks (800g)
8 thick slices crusty white bread (320g)
2 tablespoons olive oil
60g rocket, trimmed
CHILLI TOMATO JAM
1 tablespoon olive oil
2 cloves garlic, crushed
4 medium tomatoes (760g), chopped coarsely
1 tablespoon worcestershire sauce
½ cup (125ml) sweet chilli sauce
⅓ cup (75g) firmly packed brown sugar
1 tablespoon coarsely chopped fresh coriander
CARAMELISED LEEK
30g butter
1 medium leek (350g), sliced thinly
2 tablespoons brown sugar
2 tablespoons dry white wine

1 Make chilli tomato jam and caramelised leek first.
2 Cook steaks on heated oiled grill plate (or grill or barbecue) until
   browned both sides and cooked as desired.
3 Meanwhile, brush both sides of bread slices with oil; toast both
   sides under hot grill. Sandwich rocket, steaks, chilli tomato jam
   and caramelised leek between bread slices.
   CHILLI TOMATO JAM Heat oil in medium saucepan; cook garlic,
   stirring, until browned lightly. Add tomato, sauces and sugar; bring to
   a boil. Reduce heat; simmer, uncovered, about 45 minutes or until
   mixture thickens. Stand 10 minutes; stir in coriander.
   CARAMELISED LEEK Melt butter in medium frying pan; cook leek,
   stirring, until softened. Add sugar and wine; cook, stirring occasionally,
   about 20 minutes or until leek caramelises.

serves 4
per serving 35.9g fat; 3527kJ (843 cal)

grilled sausages, ratatouille and polenta triangles

PREPARATION TIME 25 MINUTES (PLUS REFRIGERATION TIME) **COOKING TIME** 25 MINUTES

You can prepare the polenta the night before and let it set overnight in the refrigerator, before cutting into triangles and grilling. You can use any sausages you like in this recipe; beef and fennel also suit the Italian qualities of this meal.

1 litre (4 cups) water
1 cup (170g) polenta
½ cup (40g) finely grated
   parmesan cheese
1 tablespoon coarsely
   chopped fresh basil
50g butter
1 tablespoon olive oil
1 small red onion (100g),
   chopped coarsely
1 medium red capsicum (200g),
   chopped coarsely
2 medium green zucchini (240g),
   chopped coarsely
2 baby eggplant (120g),
   chopped coarsely
2 medium tomatoes (380g),
   chopped coarsely
2 teaspoons sambal oelek
2 tablespoons tomato paste
½ cup (125ml) beef stock
1 tablespoon coarsely
   chopped fresh chives
8 veal and mushroom
   sausages (640g)

1 Place the water in large saucepan; bring to a boil. Add polenta in a slow, steady stream, stirring constantly. Reduce heat; simmer, stirring constantly, about 20 minutes or until polenta thickens. Stir in cheese, basil and butter. Spread polenta evenly in lightly oiled 19cm x 29cm slice pan. When cool, cover; refrigerate about 2 hours or overnight.

2 Meanwhile, heat oil in medium saucepan; cook onion and capsicum, stirring, until onion softens. Add zucchini and eggplant; cook, stirring, 3 minutes. Stir in tomato, sambal, paste and stock; bring to a boil. Reduce heat; simmer, uncovered, about 8 minutes or until mixture thickens. Stir in chives.

3 Turn polenta onto board; trim edges. Cut polenta into quarters; cut each quarter in half diagonally to form two triangles. Cook polenta triangles on heated oiled grill plate (or grill or barbecue) until browned both sides and heated through; cover to keep warm. Cook sausages on same heated oiled grill plate (or grill or barbecue) until cooked through.

4 Serve sausages on ratatouille with polenta triangles.

serves 4
per serving 55.8g fat; 3290kJ (786 cal)

chilli, tomato and capsicum steak with spirali

PREPARATION TIME 15 MINUTES **COOKING TIME** 20 MINUTES

We used spirali, a corkscrew-shaped pasta, for this recipe, but you can use any other short pasta shape, such as shells, penne or orecchiette. Rib eye, boneless sirloin or eye fillet steak are all good substitutes for rump in this recipe.

2 teaspoons chilli powder
2 teaspoons ground cumin
500g piece rump steak
1 tablespoon olive oil
375g spirali
2 cloves garlic, crushed
1 medium green capsicum
    (200g), sliced thinly
3 large egg tomatoes (270g),
    chopped coarsely
¼ cup (50g) drained
    capers, rinsed

1 Combine chilli and cumin in small bowl; sprinkle spices on both sides of steak.
2 Heat oil in medium frying pan; cook steak, uncovered, until browned both sides and cooked as desired. Remove from pan, cover with foil; stand 10 minutes.
3 Meanwhile, cook pasta in large saucepan of boiling water, uncovered, until just tender.
4 Reheat pan with meat juices. Add remaining ingredients to pan; cook, stirring, 5 minutes. Slice steak thickly; return to pan, stirring until heated through.
5 Divide drained pasta among serving plates; top with steak and sauce.

serves 4
per serving 15g fat; 2464kJ (589 cal)

vietnamese beef pho

PREPARATION TIME 10 MINUTES **COOKING TIME** 1 HOUR 15 MINUTES

Large bowls of pho are a breakfast favourite throughout Vietnam, but we like to eat it any time of day. Round, skirt or chuck steak are all suitable for this recipe. Gravy beef is also known as shin.

3 litres (12 cups) water
1kg gravy beef
1 star anise
2.5cm piece (45g)
   fresh galangal
¼ cup (60ml) soy sauce
250g bean thread noodles
1¼ cups (100g) bean sprouts
¼ cup loosely packed fresh
   coriander leaves
⅓ cup loosely packed fresh
   vietnamese mint leaves
4 green onions, sliced thinly
1 fresh long red chilli,
   sliced thinly
⅓ cup (80ml) lime juice

1 Combine the water, beef, star anise, galangal and soy sauce in large saucepan; bring to a boil. Reduce heat; simmer, covered, 30 minutes. Uncover; simmer, 30 minutes or until beef is tender.
2 Meanwhile, place noodles in medium heatproof bowl, cover with boiling water, stand until just tender; drain. Rinse under cold water; drain.
3 Combine remaining ingredients in medium bowl.
4 Remove beef from pan; reserve broth. Remove fat and sinew from beef, slice thinly. Return beef to pan; reheat until broth just comes to a boil.
5 Divide noodles among serving bowls; top with hot beef and broth then sprout mixture.

serves 6
per serving 7.6g fat;
1351kJ (323 cal)

balkan kebabs with roasted potato salad

PREPARATION TIME 25 MINUTES **COOKING TIME** 30 MINUTES

These two Croatian specialties, cevapcici, a spicy sausage, and raznjici, beef kebabs, are typical Balkan ways of cooking meat. Both are delicious, homely fare traditionally served as part of a picnic menu in summer, and eaten in home-style restaurants year round. Soak 16 small bamboo skewers in cold water for at least 1 hour before use, to prevent them from scorching and splintering.

1kg kipfler potatoes
1 tablespoon olive oil
250g mince
1 clove garlic, crushed
¼ teaspoon cayenne pepper
1 egg white, beaten lightly
2 tablespoons packaged breadcrumbs
400g rump steak, cut into 2cm cubes
1 teaspoon hot paprika
⅓ cup (95g) yogurt
1 tablespoon coarsely chopped fresh coriander
LEMON GARLIC DRESSING
¼ cup (60ml) lemon juice
2 cloves garlic, crushed
⅓ cup (80ml) olive oil
2 teaspoons dijon mustard
1 tablespoon coarsely chopped fresh coriander

1 Preheat oven to moderately hot.
2 Scrub unpeeled potatoes, dry with absorbent paper; quarter lengthways. Place potato, in single layer, in medium baking dish; drizzle with oil. Roast, uncovered, in moderately hot oven about 30 minutes or until tender.
3 Meanwhile, using hands, combine mince, garlic, pepper, egg white and breadcrumbs in medium bowl; shape mixture into eight sausages. Thread one sausage onto each of eight skewers, cover; refrigerate 15 minutes.
4 Thread rump onto eight remaining skewers; sprinkle with paprika. Cook rump and sausage skewers, in batches, on heated oiled grill plate (or grill or barbecue) until browned all over and cooked as desired.
5 Make lemon garlic dressing, pour over potato in large serving bowl; toss to combine. Combine yogurt and coriander in small bowl.
6 Serve potato salad with skewers; pass yogurt mixture separately.
   LEMON GARLIC DRESSING Combine ingredients in screw-top jar; shake well.

serves 4
per serving 38.7g fat; 2843kJ (679 cal)

tuscan beef stew

PREPARATION TIME 15 MINUTES **COOKING TIME** 2 HOURS 40 MINUTES

Round steak and skirt steak are also suitable for this recipe.

1 tablespoon olive oil
400g spring onions, trimmed
1kg chuck steak, cut into 3cm cubes
30g butter
2 tablespoons plain flour
2 cups (500ml) dry red wine
1 cup (250ml) beef stock
1 cup (250ml) water
2 cloves garlic, crushed
6 sprigs thyme
2 bay leaves
1 trimmed stick celery (75g), chopped coarsely
400g baby carrots, trimmed, halved
2 cups (250g) frozen peas
⅓ cup coarsely chopped fresh flat-leaf parsley

1 Heat oil in large heavy-based saucepan; cook onions, stirring occasionally, about 10 minutes or until browned lightly, remove from pan. Cook steak, in batches, over high heat in same pan, until browned all over.

2 Melt butter in same saucepan, add flour; cook, stirring, until mixture bubbles and thickens. Gradually stir in wine, stock and the water; stir until mixture boils and thickens. Return steak to pan with garlic, thyme and bay leaves; bring to a boil. Reduce heat; simmer, covered, 1½ hours.

3 Add onions to pan with celery and carrot; simmer, covered, 30 minutes. Add peas; simmer, uncovered, until peas are just tender. Stir in parsley just before serving.

serves 4
per serving 22.9g fat; 2500kJ (597 cal)
serving suggestion Serve with a short pasta, such as penne or farfalle.

beef and red wine casserole

PREPARATION TIME 20 MINUTES **COOKING TIME** I HOUR

Round steak and chuck steak are also suitable for this recipe.

2 cups (500ml) water
1kg skirt steak, trimmed,
 cut into 3cm cubes
2 medium brown onions (300g),
 sliced thickly
2 tablespoons olive oil
6 cloves garlic, crushed
2 cups (500ml) beef stock
2 cups (500ml) dry red wine
½ cup (140g) tomato paste
1 tablespoon finely chopped
 fresh rosemary
1 tablespoon finely chopped
 fresh flat-leaf parsley
500g fresh fettuccine

1 Combine the water, steak,
 onion, oil, garlic, stock, wine and
 paste in deep 3-litre (12 cup)
 microwave-safe dish; cook,
 covered, on HIGH (100%) for
 50 minutes, stirring every
 15 minutes to ensure steak
 remains covered in cooking
 liquid. Uncover; cook on HIGH
 (100%) about 10 minutes or until
 steak is tender. Stir in herbs.
2 During final 10 minutes of
 casserole cooking time, cook
 pasta in large saucepan of
 boiling water, uncovered,
 until just tender; drain.
3 Divide pasta among serving
 dishes; top with beef casserole.

serves 4
per serving 16.8g fat;
2795kJ (668 cal)

veal chops with pear relish and spinach

PREPARATION TIME 15 MINUTES **COOKING TIME** 55 MINUTES

4 veal chops (800g)
40g butter
400g baby spinach leaves
PEAR RELISH
4 small pears (720g)
1 medium red onion (150g),
 chopped coarsely
20g butter
1 tablespoon red wine vinegar
¼ cup (55g) firmly packed
 brown sugar
4 cloves
¼ teaspoon ground allspice

1 Make pear relish.

2 Cook chops on heated oiled grill plate (or grill or barbecue) until browned both sides and cooked as desired.

3 Meanwhile, melt butter in large saucepan; cook spinach, tossing, until just wilted.

4 Serve chops with spinach and pear relish.

PEAR RELISH Peel and core pears; chop coarsely. Combine pear in medium saucepan with onion, butter and vinegar; bring to a boil. Reduce heat; simmer, covered, about 20 minutes or until mixture is pulpy. Add sugar, cloves and allspice, stir over low heat until sugar dissolves; bring to a boil. Reduce heat; simmer, uncovered, stirring occasionally, about 20 minutes or until mixture thickens slightly.

serves 4
per serving 16.7g fat;
1731kJ (414 cal)

souvlaki with greek salad

PREPARATION TIME 30 MINUTES (PLUS MARINATING TIME) **COOKING TIME** 15 MINUTES

Souvlaki is a Greek speciality: delectably tender meat skewers which have been marinated in a herb, lemon and olive oil mixture. Rigani (Greek oregano) is a stronger, sharper version of the herb we usually associate with Italian cooking, and is available from good delicatessens and Mediterranean food stores. You can also use a piece of scotch fillet for this recipe. Soak 8 bamboo skewers in water for at least 1 hour before use to prevent scorching and splintering.

750g rump steak, cut into 2cm cubes
1 large brown onion (200g), cut into wedges
¼ cup (60ml) olive oil
¼ cup (60ml) lemon juice
1 tablespoon dried rigani

GREEK SALAD

4 medium egg tomatoes (300g), chopped coarsely
2 lebanese cucumbers (260g), chopped coarsely
1 small red onion (100g), sliced thinly
1 large green capsicum (350g), chopped coarsely
½ cup (80g) seeded kalamata olives
150g fetta cheese, chopped coarsely
1 tablespoon olive oil
1 tablespoon lemon juice
2 teaspoons fresh oregano leaves

1 Thread steak and onion alternately on skewers; place souvlaki, in single layer, in large shallow dish. Combine oil, juice and rigani in jug; pour over souvlaki. Cover; refrigerate 3 hours or overnight.
2 Make greek salad.
3 Cook souvlaki, in batches, on heated oiled grill plate (or grill or barbecue) until browned all over and cooked as desired. Serve souvlaki and greek salad with tzatziki (yogurt and cucumber salad), if desired.
GREEK SALAD Combine tomato, cucumber, onion, capsicum, olives and cheese in large bowl. Place remaining ingredients in screw-top jar; shake well. Pour dressing over salad in bowl; toss gently to combine.

serves 4
per serving 40.8g fat; 2627kJ (627 cal)

standing rib roast with roast vegetables

PREPARATION TIME 20 MINUTES **COOKING TIME** I HOUR 30 MINUTES

1.2kg standing rib roast
¼ cup (60ml) olive oil
2 teaspoons cracked black pepper
500g tiny new potatoes
500g pumpkin, chopped coarsely
500g kumara, chopped coarsely
½ cup (125ml) brandy
1½ cups (375ml) beef stock
1 tablespoon cornflour
¼ cup (60ml) water
1 tablespoon finely chopped fresh chives

1 Preheat oven to moderately hot.
2 Brush roast with 1 tablespoon of the oil; sprinkle with pepper.
  Heat 1 tablespoon of the oil in large shallow flameproof baking dish;
  cook roast, uncovered, over high heat until browned all over.
  Place dish in moderately hot oven; roast, uncovered, about
  45 minutes or until cooked as desired.
3 Meanwhile, heat remaining oil in another large flameproof baking dish;
  cook potatoes, stirring, over high heat until browned lightly. Add pumpkin
  and kumara, place dish in oven; roast, uncovered, in moderately hot
  oven about 35 minutes or until vegetables are browned.
4 Place roast on vegetables, cover; return to oven to keep warm.
  Drain juices from roast baking dish into medium saucepan, add brandy;
  bring to a boil. Add stock and blended cornflour and water; cook,
  stirring, until sauce boils and thickens slightly. Stir in chives; pour into
  medium heatproof jug.
5 Serve roast and vegetables on a large platter; accompany with sauce.

serves 4
per serving 34g fat; 3222kJ (770 cal)

sicilian stuffed pizza

PREPARATION TIME 20 MINUTES **COOKING TIME** 35 MINUTES (PLUS STANDING TIME)

Variously called sfinciuni or sfincione in Sicily, we call it delicious – a double-decker pizza with its aromatic filling hidden between the layers.

¾ cup (180ml) warm water
1½ teaspoons (7g) dried yeast
½ teaspoon sugar
2 cups (300g) plain flour
1 teaspoon salt
⅓ cup (80ml) olive oil
1 cup (70g) stale breadcrumbs
2 cloves garlic, crushed
1 teaspoon ground fennel
1 small red onion (100g), chopped finely
250g mince
100g Italian salami, chopped finely
425g can crushed tomatoes
¼ cup (40g) pine nuts, toasted
¼ cup coarsely chopped fresh flat-leaf parsley
½ cup (50g) finely grated fontina cheese

1 Combine the water, yeast and sugar in small bowl, cover; stand in warm place about 15 minutes or until frothy. Combine flour and salt in large bowl, stir in yeast mixture and half of the oil; mix to a soft dough. Turn dough onto lightly floured surface, knead about 5 minutes or until smooth and elastic. Place dough in large lightly oiled bowl, cover; stand in warm place about 1 hour or until dough doubles in size.

2 Meanwhile, heat remaining oil in large frying pan; cook breadcrumbs and half of the garlic, stirring, until crumbs are browned lightly. Remove from pan.

3 Reheat same pan; cook fennel, onion and remaining garlic, stirring, until onion just softens. Add mince; cook, stirring, until mince changes colour. Stir in salami and undrained tomatoes; bring to a boil. Reduce heat; simmer, uncovered, stirring occasionally, about 15 minutes or until liquid reduces by half. Remove from heat; stir in nuts and parsley. Cool.

4 Preheat oven to hot.

5 Knead dough on lightly floured surface until smooth; divide in half. Roll each half into 30cm round. Place one round on lightly oiled pizza or oven tray, top with breadcrumb mixture, mince mixture, cheese then remaining round. Pinch edges together; bake, uncovered, in hot oven about 15 minutes or until browned lightly.

6 Stand pizza 10 minutes before cutting into wedges and serving with a rocket and parmesan salad, if desired.

serves 4
per serving 47.7g fat; 3610kJ (862 cal)

soupe au pistou

PREPARATION TIME 15 MINUTES (PLUS SOAKING TIME) **COOKING TIME** 1 HOUR 40 MINUTES

Soupe au pistou is a classic Provençale recipe, usually made with white and green beans, and flavoured with pistou, a French spin-off of its near-neighbour Italy's pesto. Not dissimilar to Italian minestrone, this soup also benefits from being made a day in advance.

1 cup (200g) dried cannellini beans
⅓ cup (80ml) olive oil
2 veal shanks (1.5kg), trimmed
1 large leek (500g), sliced thinly
2 litres (8 cups) water
2 cups (500ml) chicken stock
2 tablespoons toasted pine nuts
1 clove garlic, quartered
¼ cup (20g) finely grated parmesan cheese
½ cup firmly packed fresh basil leaves
2 medium carrots (240g), chopped coarsely
200g green beans, trimmed, chopped coarsely

1 Cover cannellini beans with cold water in large bowl; stand, covered, overnight.
2 Heat 1 tablespoon of the oil in large saucepan; cook shanks, uncovered, until browned all over. Remove from pan. Cook leek in same pan, stirring, about 5 minutes or until just softened. Return shanks to pan with the water and stock; bring to a boil. Reduce heat; simmer, covered, 1 hour.
3 Meanwhile, blend or process remaining oil, nuts, garlic and cheese until combined. Add basil; process until pistou mixture forms a paste.
4 Remove shanks from soup. When cool enough to handle, remove meat from bones. Discard bones; chop meat coarsely. Return meat to soup with rinsed and drained cannellini beans; bring to a boil. Reduce heat; simmer, uncovered, 20 minutes. Add carrot; simmer, uncovered, 10 minutes. Add green beans and pistou; simmer, uncovered, 5 minutes.
5 Divide soup among serving bowls. Serve with slices of warm baguette, if desired, for dipping in soup.

serves 8
per serving 15g fat; 1265kJ (302 cal)

slow-roasted shanks with pumpkin and carrot risotto

PREPARATION TIME 30 MINUTES **COOKING TIME** 2 HOURS 45 MINUTES

Ask your butcher to quarter the beef shank crossways so that the pieces will fit into the baking dish.

1 large beef shank (2.5kg),
   quartered crossways
2 tablespoons plain flour
2 tablespoons olive oil
2 x 425g cans crushed tomatoes
½ cup (125ml) dry white wine
½ cup (125ml) beef stock
¼ cup (70g) tomato paste
¼ cup finely chopped fresh
   flat-leaf parsley
2 tablespoons finely chopped
   fresh lemon thyme

PUMPKIN AND CARROT RISOTTO

450g butternut pumpkin,
   chopped coarsely
2 large carrots (360g),
   chopped coarsely
2 tablespoons olive oil
1.5 litres (6 cups) chicken stock
1 cup (250ml) dry white wine
30g butter
1 medium brown onion (150g),
   chopped coarsely
2 cups (400g) arborio rice
¼ cup (20g) coarsely grated
   parmesan cheese

1 Preheat oven to very hot. Roast vegetables for risotto; when vegetables are just tender, remove from oven. Reduce oven temperature to moderate.

2 Meanwhile, toss shank pieces in flour; shake away excess. Heat oil in large frying pan; cook shank pieces, in batches, until browned and almost crunchy all over.

3 Place undrained tomatoes, wine, stock and paste in deep 5-litre (20 cup) baking dish; stir to combine. Place shank pieces, one at a time, standing upright, in dish; cook, covered, in moderate oven about 2 hours or until tender.

4 Remove shanks from dish. When cool enough to handle, remove meat from bones. Discard bones; chop meat coarsely. Return meat to dish with tomato sauce; reheat if necessary. Stir in herbs just before serving with risotto.

PUMPKIN AND CARROT RISOTTO Place pumpkin and carrot in lightly oiled large shallow baking dish, in single layer; drizzle with oil. Roast, uncovered, in very hot oven about 20 minutes or until vegetables are just tender. Remove from oven; reserve. About 40 minutes before shanks are cooked, place stock and wine in medium saucepan; bring to a boil. Reduce heat; simmer, covered. Melt butter in large saucepan; cook onion, stirring, until softened. Add rice; stir to coat in onion mixture. Stir in 1 cup of the hot stock mixture; cook, stirring, over low heat, until liquid is absorbed. Continue adding stock mixture, in 1-cup batches, stirring until absorbed after each addition. Gently stir pumpkin, carrot and cheese into risotto with last cup of stock mixture. Total cooking time should be about 35 minutes or until rice is just tender.

serves 6
per serving 36.5g fat; 3693kJ (882 cal)

vindaloo with raita and spicy dhal

PREPARATION TIME 40 MINUTES (PLUS MARINATING TIME) **COOKING TIME** 3 HOURS 20 MINUTES

Both the vindaloo curry and the spicy dhal are best made a day ahead to allow their flavours to develop fully. Round steak and skirt steak are also suitable for this recipe.

2 teaspoons cumin seeds

2 teaspoons garam masala

4 cardamom pods, bruised

1 tablespoon grated fresh ginger

6 cloves garlic, crushed

8 fresh red thai chillies,
   chopped finely

2 tablespoons white vinegar

1 tablespoon tamarind concentrate

1.5kg chuck steak, cut into 3cm cubes

2 tablespoons ghee

2 large brown onions (400g),
   chopped finely

1 cinnamon stick

6 cloves

2 teaspoons plain flour

3 cups (750ml) beef stock

SPICY DHAL

2 tablespoons vegetable oil

2 cloves garlic, crushed

1 teaspoon grated fresh ginger

1 medium brown onion (150g),
   chopped finely

3 teaspoons chilli powder

2 teaspoons sugar

2 teaspoons garam masala

2 teaspoons ground turmeric

½ teaspoon ground coriander

1 tablespoon ground cumin

1 cup (200g) red lentils

400g can crushed tomatoes

1 trimmed stick celery (75g),
   sliced thinly

2 tablespoons lemon juice

2½ cups (625ml) vegetable stock

⅓ cup (80ml) cream

2 tablespoons coarsely chopped
   fresh coriander

RAITA

1 lebanese cucumber (130g), seeded,
   grated coarsely, drained

1 small brown onion (80g),
   chopped finely

400g yogurt

¼ teaspoon chilli powder

1 teaspoon toasted black
   mustard seeds

1 tablespoon coarsely chopped
   fresh coriander

1 tablespoon coarsely chopped
   fresh mint

1 Place cumin, garam masala and cardamom in large heated dry frying pan; stir over heat until fragrant. Combine roasted spices with ginger, garlic, chilli, vinegar and tamarind in large bowl; add steak, toss to coat steak in marinade. Cover; refrigerate for 1 hour or overnight.

2 Melt ghee in same pan; cook onion, cinnamon and cloves, stirring, until onion is browned lightly. Add steak mixture; cook, stirring, until steak is browned all over. Stir in flour; cook, stirring, 2 minutes. Gradually add stock; bring to a boil, stirring. Reduce heat; simmer, uncovered, 1 hour. Serve vindaloo with spicy dhal, raita and, if desired, a bowl of crisp pappadums.

SPICY DHAL Heat oil in large heavy-based saucepan; cook garlic, ginger and onion, stirring, until onion softens. Add chilli, sugar and spices; cook, stirring, until fragrant. Add lentils, undrained tomatoes, celery, juice and stock; bring to a boil. Reduce heat; simmer, covered, about 30 minutes or until lentils are tender. Blend or process dhal mixture, in batches, until pureed; return to pan. Add cream and coriander; cook, stirring, until heated through.

RAITA Combine ingredients in medium bowl.

serves 4

per serving 52.3g fat; 4428kJ (1058 cal)

teriyaki steak

PREPARATION TIME 10 MINUTES (PLUS MARINATING TIME) **COOKING TIME** 10 MINUTES

You can also use scotch fillet in this recipe if you like.

750g piece rump steak, sliced thinly
¼ cup (60ml) rice vinegar
¼ cup (60ml) kecap manis
1 tablespoon brown sugar
¼ cup (60ml) lime juice
1 clove garlic, crushed
2 small fresh red chillies, seeded,
    chopped finely
1 teaspoon sesame oil
1 tablespoon peanut oil
1 large carrot (180g),
    cut into matchsticks
200g cabbage, shredded finely
¼ cup (50g) japanese
    pickled cucumber

1 Combine steak, vinegar, kecap manis, sugar, juice, garlic, chilli and sesame oil in large bowl, cover; refrigerate 3 hours or overnight. Drain steak; reserve marinade.

2 Heat peanut oil in wok or large frying pan; stir-fry steak, in batches, until browned all over. Cover steak to keep warm.

3 Pour reserved marinade into wok; bring to a boil. Boil, uncovered, until sauce reduces by a third. Divide combined carrot and cabbage among serving plates; top with steak, drizzle with sauce. Serve with pickles and, if desired, steamed koshihikari rice.

serves 4
per serving 18.6g fat;
1636kJ (391 cal)
tips Japanese pickled cucumber has a sour taste and is available, packaged in brine, from most Asian food stores.

ravioli with caramelised fennel and leek

PREPARATION TIME 30 MINUTES **COOKING TIME** 25 MINUTES

80g butter
2 tablespoons olive oil
1 large fennel (450g), trimmed,
  sliced thinly
1 large leek (500g), chopped finely
⅓ cup (80ml) dry white wine
1 tablespoon sugar
300g mince
270g packet wonton wrappers
1 egg, beaten lightly
2 tablespoons lemon juice
1 clove garlic, crushed
1 tablespoon finely chopped
  fresh chives

1 Heat a quarter of the butter with
   half of the oil in large non-stick frying
   pan; cook fennel and leek, stirring,
   5 minutes. Stir in wine and sugar;
   bring to a boil. Reduce heat; simmer,
   covered, stirring occasionally, about
   20 minutes or until liquid is absorbed
   and vegetables are caramelised.
2 Meanwhile, combine mince with
   remaining oil in medium bowl.
3 Place a heaped teaspoon of mince
   mixture in centre of one wrapper,
   brush edges with a little egg; top
   with another wrapper, press edges
   together to seal. Repeat with remaining
   mince mixture, wrappers and egg.
4 Cook ravioli, in batches, in large
   saucepan of boiling water,
   uncovered, until ravioli float to the
   surface, wrappers are tender and
   mince is cooked through; drain.
   Toss ravioli in large bowl with
   remaining chopped butter, juice
   and garlic.
5 Divide ravioli among serving bowls;
   top with caramelised fennel and
   leek; sprinkle with chives.

serves 4
per serving 36.1g fat;
2246kJ (537 cal)

fajitas and guacamole

PREPARATION TIME 15 MINUTES (PLUS MARINATING TIME) **COOKING TIME** 20 MINUTES

Tex-Mex cooking is responsible for spreading the popularity of fajitas among beef-lovers around the world. While the marinade can be made of a wide variety of ingredients, there are two requisites for any fajita recipe: it must always include capsicums of more than one colour and should always be accompanied by guacamole. Scotch fillet bought in a large piece is also known as rib-eye roast; you can also use rump for this recipe.

600g piece scotch fillet
2 cloves garlic, crushed
¼ cup (60ml) lemon juice
1½ teaspoons ground cumin
½ teaspoon cayenne pepper
2 tablespoons olive oil
1 medium yellow capsicum (200g)
1 medium red capsicum (200g)
12 small flour tortillas
375g jar chunky salsa
GUACAMOLE
2 medium avocados (500g)
2 medium tomatoes (380g), seeded, chopped finely
1 small red onion (100g), chopped finely
2 tablespoons lime juice
2 tablespoons coarsely chopped fresh coriander

1   Cut fillet into thin 2cm-wide slices; place in medium bowl with garlic, juice, spices and oil, toss to coat fillet in marinade. Cover; refrigerate for 3 hours.

2   Quarter capsicums; remove seeds and membranes. Roast capsicum under grill or in very hot oven, skin-side up, until skin blisters and blackens. Cover with plastic or paper for 5 minutes. Peel away skin; cut capsicums into thin strips.

3   Cook fillet, in batches, on heated oiled grill plate (or grill or barbecue) until browned all over and cooked as desired; cover to keep warm. Reheat capsicum strips on same heated grill.

4   Serve fillet and capsicum immediately, accompanied by guacamole, tortillas and salsa.
    GUACAMOLE Mash avocados roughly in medium bowl; add remaining ingredients, mix to combine.

serves 4
per serving 48.8g fat; 4097kJ (979 cal)

fillet steak, cheese and capsicum stacks with parmesan mash

PREPARATION TIME 20 MINUTES **COOKING TIME** 15 MINUTES

1 medium red capsicum (200g)
1kg potatoes, chopped coarsely
4 fillet steaks (500g)
4 thick slices gouda cheese (125g)
20g baby spinach leaves
¼ cup (60ml) cream
20g butter
½ cup (40g) finely grated parmesan cheese
400g sugar snap peas

1 Quarter capsicum; remove seeds and membranes. Roast capsicum under grill or in very hot oven, skin-side up, until skin blisters and blackens. Cover with plastic or paper for 5 minutes. Peel away skin.

2 Meanwhile, boil, steam or microwave potatoes until tender; drain. Cover to keep warm.

3 Preheat oven to hot.

4 Cut steaks in half horizontally; divide gouda cheese, spinach and capsicum among four steak halves, cover with remaining steak halves. Tie stacks with kitchen string; cook, uncovered, in lightly oiled large non-stick frying pan until browned both sides. Transfer to oven tray; cook, uncovered, in hot oven about 10 minutes or until cooked as desired.

5 Meanwhile, mash potatoes with cream, butter and parmesan cheese until smooth. Boil, steam or microwave peas until just tender; drain.

6 Serve stacks with parmesan mash and peas.

serves 4
per serving 31.4g fat; 2568kJ (613 cal)

borscht with meatballs

PREPARATION TIME 20 MINUTES **COOKING TIME** 2 HOURS

Borscht is a fresh beetroot soup, originally from Poland and Russia,
made with meat or cabbage, or both. Serve it cold or hot, but always
with a dollop of sour cream. Ask your butcher to cut the shanks
into thirds for you.

1 tablespoon olive oil
1 small brown onion (80g), chopped coarsely
1 small carrot (70g), chopped coarsely
1 small leek (200g), chopped coarsely
250g cabbage, chopped coarsely
1 large tomato (250g), chopped coarsely
2 medium beetroots (350g), peeled, chopped coarsely
2 veal shanks (1.5kg), trimmed, cut into thirds
1.25 litres (5 cups) water
500g mince
½ cup (100g) medium-grain white rice
1 teaspoon sweet paprika
1 small brown onion (80g), chopped finely
3 cloves garlic, crushed
½ cup finely chopped fresh flat-leaf parsley
2 eggs, beaten lightly
½ cup (120g) sour cream
2 tablespoons finely chopped fresh dill

1 Heat oil in large saucepan; cook coarsely chopped onion, carrot,
leek, cabbage, tomato and beetroot, stirring, 15 minutes. Add shank
and the water; bring to a boil. Reduce heat; simmer, covered,
1½ hours. Remove shank; remove and reserve meat from shank
for another use, if desired.
2 Meanwhile, using hands, combine mince, rice, paprika, finely chopped
onion, garlic, parsley and egg in large bowl; shape rounded teaspoons
of mince mixture into meatballs.
3 Return borscht to a boil; add meatballs. Reduce heat; simmer,
uncovered, until meatballs are cooked through.
4 Divide borscht and meatballs among serving bowls; dollop with combined
sour cream and dill. Serve with sliced rye or pumpernickel bread.

serves 4
per serving 36g fat; 3187kJ (761 cal)
tips Make the meatballs the day before; refrigerate them, uncooked,
covered on a tray. Drop meatballs in reheated soup to cook.
Make soup a day ahead to allow the flavours to intensify.

green chilli stew

PREPARATION TIME 15 MINUTES **COOKING TIME** 1 HOUR 40 MINUTES

Round steak, skirt steak and gravy beef are also suitable for this recipe.

2 tablespoons olive oil
1kg chuck steak, cut into 3cm cubes
1 large brown onion (200g), sliced thinly
2 cloves garlic, sliced thinly
2 teaspoons ground cumin
2 fresh long green chillies, seeded, sliced thinly
2 cups (500ml) beef stock
1 tablespoon tomato paste
3 large egg tomatoes (270g), chopped coarsely
500g tiny new potatoes, halved
4 small flour tortillas
¼ cup coarsely chopped fresh coriander

1 Heat half of the oil in large flameproof baking dish; cook steak, in batches, stirring, until browned all over.
2 Preheat oven to moderate.
3 Heat remaining oil in same dish; cook onion, garlic, cumin and chilli, stirring, until onion softens. Add stock and paste; bring to a boil, stirring. Return steak to dish; cook, covered, in moderate oven 45 minutes.
4 Add tomato and potato; cook, covered, in moderate oven 35 minutes. Uncover; cook 20 minutes.
5 Meanwhile, cut each tortilla into six wedges. Place, in single layer, on oven trays; toast, uncovered, in moderate oven about 8 minutes or until crisp.
6 Stir coriander into stew just before serving with tortilla crisps and, if desired, grilled cobs of corn.

serves 4
per serving 24.7g fat; 2740kJ (655 cal)
tip Tortilla crisps can be prepared up to two days ahead and kept in an airtight container at room temperature.

carpaccio with fennel salad

PREPARATION TIME 10 MINUTES (PLUS FREEZING TIME)

400g piece eye fillet
2 medium bulbs fennel (600g)
2 trimmed sticks celery (150g)
2 tablespoons finely chopped
   fresh flat-leaf parsley
2 tablespoons lemon juice
1 clove garlic, crushed
¼ teaspoon sugar
½ teaspoon dijon mustard
⅓ cup (80ml) olive oil

1 Remove any excess fat from
fillet, wrap tightly in plastic wrap;
freeze about 1 hour or until
partially frozen. Using sharp knife,
slice fillet as thinly as possible.
2 Meanwhile, slice fennel and
celery finely. Toss in medium
bowl with remaining ingredients.
3 Arrange carpaccio slices in
single layer on serving plates;
top with fennel salad. Serve
accompanied with sliced
Italian bread.

serves 4
per serving 25.2g fat;
1404kJ (335 cal)

veal goulash with braised red cabbage

PREPARATION TIME 20 MINUTES **COOKING TIME** I HOUR 30 MINUTES

1 tablespoon olive oil
1 medium brown onion (150g),
    sliced thickly
1 medium red capsicum (200g),
    sliced thickly
2 cloves garlic, crushed
800g boneless veal leg,
    cut into 3cm cubes
1 tablespoon sweet paprika
½ teaspoon cayenne pepper
425g can crushed tomatoes
1½ cups (375ml) beef stock
1 cup (200g) long-grain
    brown rice
30g butter
400g red cabbage,
    chopped coarsely

1 Heat oil in large saucepan; cook onion, capsicum and garlic until onion softens. Add veal, paprika, pepper, undrained tomato and ½ cup of the stock; bring to a boil, stirring. Reduce heat; simmer, uncovered, about 1 hour or until veal is tender and sauce thickens slightly.
2 Meanwhile, cook rice in medium saucepan of boiling water until just tender; drain.
3 Melt butter in large frying pan; cook cabbage, stirring, about 5 minutes or until just softened. Add remaining stock; bring to a boil. Reduce heat; simmer, covered, 10 minutes.
4 Serve goulash with rice and braised red cabbage.

serves 4
per serving 14g fat;
2242kJ (536 cal)

wiener schnitzel with lemon spaetzle

PREPARATION TIME 20 MINUTES (PLUS REFRIGERATION TIME) **COOKING TIME** 20 MINUTES

Spaetzle, served throughout Germany, Austria, Switzerland and the French region of Alsace, are tiny noodle-like dumplings made by pushing a batter through the holes of a colander or strainer into a pan of boiling water or stock. The cooked spaetzle are generally tossed in a frying pan with melted butter, herbs or gravy then served as a side dish, or added to soups or stews in place of pasta or potatoes.

½ cup (75g) plain flour
3 eggs, beaten lightly
2 tablespoons milk
2 cups (140g) stale breadcrumbs
¾ cup (75g) packaged breadcrumbs
½ cup (40g) finely grated parmesan cheese
8 veal schnitzels (800g)
vegetable oil, for shallow-frying
LEMON SPAETZLE
2 cups (300g) plain flour
4 eggs, beaten lightly
½ cup (125ml) water
2 teaspoons finely grated lemon rind
40g butter, chopped

1 Whisk flour, egg and milk in medium shallow bowl; combine breadcrumbs and cheese in another medium shallow bowl. Coat schnitzels, one at a time, in flour mixture then in breadcrumb mixture. Place, in single layer, on tray. Cover; refrigerate 15 minutes.
2 Make lemon spaetzle.
3 Heat oil in large frying pan; cook schnitzels, in batches, until browned both sides and cooked through.
4 Serve schnitzel with lemon spaetzle.
   LEMON SPAETZLE Place flour in large bowl, make well in centre. Gradually add egg and the water, stirring, until batter is smooth. Stir in rind. Pour half of the batter into metal colander set over large saucepan of boiling water; using wooden spoon, push batter through holes of colander, remove colander. When water returns to a boil, boil, uncovered, about 2 minutes or until spaetzle float to the surface. Use slotted spoon to remove spaetzle; drain, place in large bowl. Add half of the butter; toss spaetzle gently until butter melts. Keep warm; repeat with remaining batter and butter.

serves 4
per serving 58.1g fat; 5245kJ (1253 cal)

veal loin with baked figs and port sauce

PREPARATION TIME 10 MINUTES (PLUS MARINATING TIME) **COOKING TIME** 50 MINUTES

This cut of veal includes the tenderloin of veal, which is very pale in colour (almost white), is trimmed of any excess fat, and has a firm, velvety texture.

800g piece boneless loin of veal roast
¼ cup (60ml) balsamic vinegar
2 tablespoons olive oil
1 clove garlic, crushed
9 medium fresh figs (540g), halved
1 litre (4 cups) water
3 cups (750ml) milk
1½ cups (255g) instant polenta
40g butter
½ cup (125ml) cream
4 green onions, chopped finely
½ cup coarsely chopped fresh flat-leaf parsley
⅓ cup (80ml) port
1 cup (250ml) beef stock
1 tablespoon cornflour
¼ cup (60ml) water, extra

1 Place veal in large bowl with combined vinegar, oil and garlic; coat veal all over in marinade. Cover; refrigerate 3 hours or overnight.
2 Preheat oven to moderately hot.
3 Drain veal; discard marinade. Heat large flameproof baking dish; cook veal, uncovered, until browned all over. Roast, uncovered, in moderately hot oven 30 minutes. Stir in fig halves; roast, uncovered, in moderately hot oven about 10 minutes or until figs are just tender.
4 Meanwhile, combine the water and milk in large saucepan; bring to a boil. Add polenta in a slow, steady stream, stirring constantly. Reduce heat; simmer, stirring constantly, about 20 minutes or until polenta thickens. Stir in butter, cream, onion and parsley.
5 Remove veal and figs from baking dish; cover to keep warm. Place dish with pan juices over high heat, add port; bring to a boil. Cook, stirring, 2 minutes. Add stock; bring to a boil. Cook, uncovered, 3 minutes. Add blended cornflour and extra water; cook, stirring, until sauce boils and thickens.
6 Serve veal on polenta, topped with figs and drizzled with sauce.

serves 6
per serving 28.9g fat; 2602kJ (621 cal)

barbecued short ribs and potato pancakes

PREPARATION TIME 25 MINUTES (PLUS MARINATING TIME) **COOKING TIME** 3 HOURS 10 MINUTES

Beef short ribs are slabs of meat, fat and bone, measuring about 5cm by 8cm, usually cut from between the neck and shoulder. They need slow, moist cooking to be at their most delectable. Ask your butcher to cut them for you in advance.

2 tablespoons vegetable oil

1 medium brown onion (150g), chopped coarsely

3 cloves garlic, crushed

½ cup (125ml) dry red wine

¼ cup (55g) firmly packed brown sugar

2 tablespoons dijon mustard

2 tablespoons worcestershire sauce

425g can crushed tomatoes

2kg short ribs

POTATO PANCAKES

2 medium potatoes (400g), grated coarsely

⅓ cup (50g) self-raising flour

¼ teaspoon ground nutmeg

3 eggs, beaten lightly

½ cup (125ml) buttermilk

1 tablespoon finely chopped fresh chives

2 egg whites

30g butter

1 tablespoon vegetable oil

1 Heat oil in small saucepan; cook onion and garlic, stirring, until onion softens. Stir in wine, sugar, mustard, sauce and undrained tomatoes; bring to a boil. Reduce heat; simmer barbecue sauce, uncovered, 5 minutes, cool. Reserve half of the barbecue sauce; store, covered, in refrigerator.

2 Using kitchen scissors, separate ribs; place in large bowl with remaining barbecue sauce; toss ribs to coat all over with sauce. Cover; refrigerate 3 hours or overnight.

3 Preheat oven to slow.

4 Drain ribs; reserve marinade. Place ribs, in single layer, in large shallow baking dish. Cook, covered, in slow oven about 1½ hours, brushing occasionally with reserved marinade; uncover, cook in slow oven about 1 hour or until meat on ribs is tender.

5 Heat reserved barbecue sauce; bring to a boil. Reduce heat; simmer, uncovered, about 30 minutes or until sauce thickens. Blend or process sauce until smooth.

6 Serve ribs, drizzled with hot barbecue sauce, with potato pancakes. POTATO PANCAKES Pat dry potatoes with absorbent paper. Place flour and nutmeg in medium bowl; gradually whisk in eggs and buttermilk, stir in potato and chives. Place egg whites in small bowl; beat with electric mixer until soft peaks form; fold into batter. Heat butter and oil in medium heavy-based frying pan; pour approximately ¼-cup amounts of the batter, in batches, into pan; cook until browned both sides and tender.

serves 4
per serving 54.3g fat; 4343kJ (1038 cal)

hearty beef stew with red wine and mushrooms

PREPARATION TIME 10 MINUTES **COOKING TIME** 2 HOURS 50 MINUTES

The rich combination of stock and wine, plus the long, slow cooking time, gives this stew its robust intensity. Rump or round steak are also suitable for this recipe.

2 tablespoons olive oil
1.5kg blade steak, cut into 2cm cubes
1 large brown onion (200g), sliced thickly
2 cloves garlic, crushed
250g mushrooms, quartered
2 trimmed sticks celery (150g), sliced thickly
2 x 425g cans crushed tomatoes
½ cup (125ml) dry red wine
1½ cups (375ml) beef stock
2 medium potatoes (400g), quartered
2 large carrots (360g), sliced thickly
2 teaspoons coarsely chopped fresh thyme
200g green beans, trimmed
200g yellow beans, trimmed

1 Heat half of the oil in large heavy-based saucepan; cook steak, in batches, over high heat until browned all over.
2 Heat remaining oil in same pan; cook onion and garlic, stirring, until onion softens. Add mushrooms and celery; cook, stirring, 3 minutes. Return steak to pan with undrained tomatoes, wine and stock; bring to a boil. Reduce heat; simmer, covered, 2 hours.
3 Add potato and carrot; simmer, covered, about 30 minutes or until steak is tender. Stir in thyme.
4 Meanwhile, boil, steam or microwave beans until just tender; drain.
5 Serve stew with beans and, if desired, a warmed loaf of ciabatta.

serves 4
per serving 35.2g fat; 3458kJ (826 cal)

lasagne with four cheeses

PREPARATION TIME 25 MINUTES **COOKING TIME** 55 MINUTES

2 teaspoons olive oil
1 medium brown onion (150g), chopped finely
2 cloves garlic, crushed
500g lean mince
2 x 425g cans crushed tomatoes
½ cup (140g) tomato paste
½ teaspoon sugar
½ cup finely chopped fresh basil
¼ cup finely chopped fresh oregano
500g ricotta
1 cup (80g) finely grated parmesan cheese
1 cup (100g) coarsely grated mozzarella cheese
¼ teaspoon ground nutmeg
4 eggs
200g large curly instant lasagne sheets
1 cup (100g) pizza cheese

1 Heat oil in large saucepan; cook onion and garlic, stirring, until onion softens. Add mince; cook, stirring, until mince changes colour. Add undrained tomatoes, paste and sugar; cook, stirring, until sauce thickens. Remove from heat; stir in basil and oregano.
2 Preheat oven to moderate.
3 Beat ricotta, parmesan, mozzarella and nutmeg in medium bowl with electric mixer until well combined. Add eggs, one at a time, beating until just combined between additions.
4 Place a third of the lasagne sheets in shallow 2.5-litre (10 cup) baking dish; top with half of the meat sauce and half of the cheese mixture. Top with another third of the lasagne sheets, remaining meat sauce, remaining lasagne sheets then remaining cheese mixture. Top with pizza cheese.
5 Bake, uncovered, in moderate oven, about 45 minutes or until top browns lightly. Stand lasagne 5 minutes before serving.

serves 6
per serving 32.7g fat; 2620kJ (626 cal)

kofta with fresh green onion couscous

PREPARATION TIME 20 MINUTES (PLUS REFRIGERATION TIME) **COOKING TIME** 15 MINUTES

Soak 12 bamboo skewers in cold water for at least one hour before use to prevent scorching and splintering.

1kg mince
1 medium brown onion (150g), chopped finely
2 cloves garlic, crushed
2 tablespoons lemon juice
1½ teaspoons ground cumin
1½ teaspoons ground coriander
¼ cup (40g) toasted pine nuts
2 tablespoons finely chopped fresh mint
1 tablespoon finely chopped fresh coriander
1 egg
2 cups (500ml) beef stock
2 cups (400g) couscous
30g butter, chopped
2 green onions, sliced thinly

1 Using hands, combine mince, onion, garlic, juice, spices, nuts, herbs and egg in large bowl; roll heaped tablespoons of mixture into balls, thread three balls on each skewer. Place kofta skewers on tray, cover; refrigerate 30 minutes.
2 Place stock in medium saucepan; bring to a boil. Remove from heat, add couscous and butter, cover; stand about 5 minutes or until stock is absorbed, fluffing with fork occasionally.
3 Meanwhile, cook kofta on heated oiled grill plate (or grill or barbecue) until browned all over and cooked through.
4 Toss green onion with couscous; serve with kofta, accompanied by a bowl of combined yogurt and chopped cucumber, if desired.

serves 4
per serving 42.7g fat; 4114kJ (983 cal)

balti biryani

PREPARATION TIME 20 MINUTES (PLUS MARINATING TIME) **COOKING TIME** I HOUR 30 MINUTES

This delectable Indian recipe combines rice and meat with a heady mixture of aromatic spices. Biryanis are traditionally saved for special occasions, but this version is simple enough to prepare at any time. Round steak, chuck steak or gravy beef are also suitable for this recipe.

750g skirt steak, cut into 2cm cubes
¾ cup (225g) balti curry paste
2 cups (400g) basmati rice
8 cloves garlic, unpeeled
20g ghee
4 cardamom pods, bruised
4 cloves
1 cinnamon stick
3 green onions, sliced thinly
2 cups (500ml) beef stock
¾ cup (100g) toasted slivered almonds
¼ cup loosely packed fresh coriander leaves
2 fresh red thai chillies, sliced thinly

1 Preheat oven to moderate.
2 Combine steak and curry paste in medium bowl, cover; refrigerate 1 hour.
3 Meanwhile, place rice in medium bowl, cover with water; stand 30 minutes. Drain rice in strainer; rinse under cold water, drain.
4 Meanwhile, place garlic in small baking dish; roast, uncovered, in moderate oven about 20 minutes or until softened.
5 Melt ghee in large saucepan; cook cardamom, cloves, cinnamon and onion, stirring, until fragrant. Add steak mixture, reduce heat; simmer, covered, stirring occasionally, about 45 minutes or until steak is tender.
6 Add rice with stock to pan; simmer, covered, stirring occasionally, about 15 minutes or until rice is just tender.
7 Peel garlic; chop finely. Add garlic, almonds and coriander to biryani, cover; stand 5 minutes. Sprinkle biryani with chilli; serve with raita and naan, if desired.

serves 4
per serving 41.9g fat; 4016kJ (959 cal)

massaman curry

PREPARATION TIME 25 MINUTES **COOKING TIME** 1 HOUR 45 MINUTES

Having a spicy flavour reminiscent of many Middle-Eastern dishes, this curry is a Thai take on the foods introduced by Muslim traders from India and Pakistan. It remains the curry favoured by the Muslim communities of southern Thailand because it uses beef rather than pork. Round steak, chuck steak and gravy beef are also suitable for this recipe.

¼ cup (60ml) peanut oil
1kg skirt steak, cut into 4cm cubes
500g tiny new potatoes, halved
1⅔ cups (400ml) coconut cream
1 teaspoon tamarind concentrate
⅔ cup (160ml) hot water
2 tablespoons brown sugar

MASSAMAN PASTE

1 tablespoon coriander seeds
1 tablespoon cumin seeds
3 cardamom pods, bruised
½ teaspoon ground nutmeg
¼ teaspoon ground clove
¼ teaspoon black peppercorns
3 green onions, sliced thinly
2 cloves garlic, quartered
2 tablespoons finely chopped fresh lemon grass
2 fresh red thai chillies, chopped coarsely
2 teaspoons shrimp paste
2 tablespoons warm water

1 Make massaman paste first.
2 Heat oil in large saucepan; cook steak, in batches, stirring, until browned all over. Drain on absorbent paper.
3 Cook potato in same pan, stirring, until browned lightly. Stir in massaman paste; cook, stirring, 1 minute.
4 Stir in coconut cream, steak and blended tamarind, water and sugar; bring to a boil. Reduce heat; simmer, uncovered, about 1½ hours or until steak is tender and curry sauce thickens. Serve sprinkled with finely sliced red chillies and accompanied by steamed jasmine rice, if desired.
MASSAMAN PASTE Preheat oven to hot. Using mortar and pestle, crush coriander, cumin, cardamom, nutmeg, clove and peppercorns. Place on oven tray with onion, garlic, lemon grass and chilli; roast in hot oven about 5 minutes or until fragrant. Blend or process mixture with the shrimp paste and the water until smooth.

serves 4
per serving 41.5g fat; 3118kJ (745 cal)

veal escalopes with rocket and pistachio pesto

PREPARATION TIME 10 MINUTES (PLUS MARINATING TIME)   **COOKING TIME** 15 MINUTES

600g piece veal rump, sliced thinly
1 tablespoon olive oil
¼ cup (60ml) dry white wine
2 teaspoons finely grated lemon rind
1 clove garlic, crushed
375g fettuccine
ROCKET AND PISTACHIO PESTO
50g baby rocket leaves, trimmed
½ cup (75g) shelled pistachios, toasted
⅓ cup (25g) coarsely grated parmesan cheese
1 clove garlic, quartered
1 tablespoon lemon juice
¾ cup (180ml) olive oil

1 Combine veal, oil, wine, rind and garlic in medium bowl; toss to coat veal all over in marinade. Cover; refrigerate 2 hours.
2 Cook pasta in large saucepan of boiling water, uncovered, until just tender.
3 Meanwhile, cook veal, in batches, on heated oiled grill plate (or grill or barbecue) until browned all over and cooked as desired.
4 Combine drained pasta in large bowl with half of the pesto; toss gently to combine. Serve veal on pasta topped with remaining pesto; accompany with a mixed-leaf salad, if desired.
ROCKET AND PISTACHIO PESTO Blend or process rocket, nuts, cheese and garlic until well combined. With motor operating, gradually add combined juice and oil in thin stream until pesto thickens slightly.

serves 4
per serving 62.8g fat; 4435kJ (1059 cal)
tip Pesto can be made up to a week ahead and kept, covered, in the refrigerator. Pesto can also be frozen for up to 3 months.

sri lankan spicy ribs with coconut pilaf

PREPARATION TIME 20 MINUTES (PLUS MARINATING TIME) **COOKING TIME** 35 MINUTES

Order american-style spare ribs in advance from the butcher.

1.6kg american-style spare ribs
¼ cup (60ml) peanut oil
¼ cup (60ml) white vinegar
1 teaspoon sambal oelek
1 teaspoon ground turmeric
4 cloves
½ teaspoon ground cardamom
3 cloves garlic, crushed
2 teaspoons grated fresh ginger
1 small brown onion (80g), chopped finely

COCONUT PILAF
40g butter
1 medium brown onion (150g), chopped coarsely
1 medium carrot (120g), chopped coarsely
2 cups (400g) basmati rice, washed, drained
1 litre (4 cups) chicken stock
¼ cup firmly packed fresh coriander leaves
¼ cup (10g) flaked coconut
¼ cup (40g) raisins

1 Using kitchen scissors, separate ribs into sections; place in large bowl with combined oil, vinegar, sambal, turmeric, cloves, cardamom, garlic, ginger and onion. Toss ribs to coat all over in marinade, cover; refrigerate 3 hours or overnight.
2 Preheat oven to very hot.
3 Drain ribs; reserve marinade. Place ribs on wire rack over large shallow baking dish. Roast ribs, uncovered, in very hot oven, brushing frequently with reserved marinade, about 30 minutes or until browned and cooked through, turning once halfway through cooking time.
4 Serve ribs on coconut pilaf.
COCONUT PILAF Heat butter in medium saucepan; cook onion and carrot, stirring, until onion softens. Add rice; cook, stirring, 1 minute. Add stock; bring to a boil. Reduce heat; simmer, covered, about 20 minutes or until rice is just tender. Remove from heat; fluff rice with fork. Stir in coriander, coconut and raisins, cover; stand 5 minutes before serving.

serves 4
per serving 49g fat; 4604kJ (1100 cal)

beef, tomato and pea pies

PREPARATION TIME 15 MINUTES (PLUS REFRIGERATION TIME)   **COOKING TIME** 45 MINUTES

1 tablespoon vegetable oil
1 small brown onion (80g), chopped finely
300g mince
400g can crushed tomatoes
1 tablespoon tomato paste
2 tablespoons worcestershire sauce
½ cup (125ml) beef stock
½ cup (60g) frozen peas
3 sheets ready-rolled puff pastry
1 egg, beaten lightly

1   Heat oil in large saucepan; cook onion, stirring, until softened. Add mince; cook, stirring, until changed in colour. Stir in undrained tomatoes, paste, sauce and stock; bring to a boil. Reduce heat; simmer, uncovered, about 20 minutes or until sauce thickens. Stir in peas. Cool.

2   Preheat oven to moderately hot. Oil 6-hole Texas (¾ cup/180ml) muffin pan.

3   Cut two 13cm rounds from opposite corners of each pastry sheet; cut two 9cm rounds from remaining corners of each sheet. Place the six large rounds in muffin pan holes to cover bases and sides; trim any excess pastry. Lightly prick bases with fork; refrigerate 30 minutes. Cover the six small rounds with a damp cloth.

4   Cover pastry-lined muffin pan holes with baking paper; fill holes with uncooked rice or dried beans. Bake, uncovered, in moderately hot oven, 10 minutes; remove paper and rice. Cool.

5   Spoon mince filling into holes; brush edges with a little egg. Top pies with small pastry rounds; gently press around edges to seal.

6   Brush pies with remaining egg; bake, uncovered, in moderately hot oven about 15 minutes or until browned lightly. Stand 5 minutes in pan before serving with mashed potatoes, if desired.

makes 6
per serving 14g fat; 961kJ (230 cal)

fillet steaks with chilli wedges and red capsicum sauce

PREPARATION TIME 20 MINUTES **COOKING TIME** 40 MINUTES

4 large potatoes (1.2kg), cut into wedges

1 teaspoon dried chilli flakes

2 tablespoons olive oil

4 bacon rashers (280g)

4 fillet steaks (500g)

RED CAPSICUM SAUCE

2 medium red capsicums (400g)

1 tablespoon olive oil

1 medium brown onion (150g), chopped coarsely

3 cloves garlic, crushed

425g can crushed tomatoes

1 tablespoon balsamic vinegar

1 Preheat oven to hot. Make red capsicum sauce.

2 Meanwhile, place potato, in single layer, in large shallow baking dish; drizzle with combined chilli and half of the oil; roast, uncovered, in hot oven, turning occasionally, about 20 minutes or until browned all over.

3 Remove rind from bacon; wrap one rasher around circumference of each steak, trim to fit, secure with toothpick.

4 Heat remaining oil in large heavy-based frying pan; cook steak until browned both sides and cooked as desired.

5 Serve steaks with chilli wedges and red capsicum sauce.
RED CAPSICUM SAUCE Quarter capsicums; remove seeds and membranes. Roast capsicum under grill or in very hot oven, skin-side up, until skin blisters and blackens. Cover with plastic or paper for 5 minutes. Peel away skin; chop capsicum coarsely. Heat oil in medium saucepan; cook onion and garlic, stirring, until onion softens. Add capsicum with undrained tomatoes and vinegar; bring to a boil. Reduce heat; simmer, uncovered, stirring occasionally, about 20 minutes or until sauce thickens. Blend or process, in batches, until mixture is pureed.

serves 4
per serving 42.3g fat; 3202kJ (765 cal)

the brief on beef

Read on for the essential information on beef preparation, hygiene, refrigeration and freezing, and how to cook this succulent meat to perfection.

PURCHASING AND STORING

Allow 125g to 150g of lean boneless meat per person.

When shopping, take an insulated bag for meat products, making sure these are the last items purchased. Once home, refrigerate or freeze all meat products immediately.

Meat should be bright red in colour and have a fresh appearance. Select lean meat; whatever fat there is should be pale cream in colour.

Meat should be kept as dry as possible and never allowed to sit in its own juice. Cold air should be able to circulate freely around the piece of meat.

The more cutting and preparation the meat has been subjected to, the briefer the allowable storage time. This is why storage time for mince (ground) meat is less than for steaks.

If meat is to be used within 24 hours of purchase, it can be left in its original wrapping. However, if you want to keep it longer than a day, place it in a non-plastic container covered loosely with foil to allow some air-flow.

Meat that has been stored under refrigeration for 2 to 3 days will be more tender than meat cooked on the day of purchase. This is due to natural enzymes softening the muscle fibre.

Maximum refrigeration time for meat	
Mince (ground) meat and sausages	2 days
Diced meat	3 days
Steaks, chops and cutlets	4 days
Roasting joints (bone in)	3 days
Roasting joints (boned and rolled)	2 days
Silverside	1 week

HYGIENE

Careful attention to hygiene when handling meat is essential. Most cases of food poisoning result from food being unrefrigerated: the longer that any meat, raw or cooked, stands at room temperature, the greater the chance of food poisoning.

Wash your hands and utensils thoroughly before and after handling meat.

Never handle cooked and uncooked meat together; don't cut them with the same utensils or on the same chopping board.

Store cooked meat above raw meat in the refrigerator, so that there is no chance that uncooked juices can drip onto cooked meat.

Defrost frozen meat in the refrigerator before cooking – never at room temperature.

Refrigerate leftover cooked meat as soon as possible, and always reheat it to steaming hot before serving a second time.

ROASTS

Meat can be elevated over a roasting pan, either on a rack or over a bed of vegetables. The vegetables will also add flavour to the meat juices that collect in the pan.

The roast should rest before carving, allowing juices to settle in the meat.

When carving, slice across the grain. This shortens the fibre, making the slices more tender.

Weigh meat to be able to accurately calculate the cooking time.

For accuracy, use a meat thermometer. Calculate the cooking time then insert the thermometer into the thickest part of the meat at the beginning of the cooking time.

Rare = 60°C/140°F
Medium = 65-70°C/150-160°F
Well done = 75°C/170°F

CASSEROLES AND CURRIES

Seal meat in a preheated pan over high heat, in small batches, to lock in juices and develop colour.

Once liquid is added, allow the casserole to return to a boil then immediately reduce heat. Cover and simmer until tender, stirring occasionally to prevent sticking.

Don't allow a casserole or curry to boil rapidly because doing so will toughen the meat considerably. Lower heat after initially bringing the casserole or curry to a boil, then cook it over a simmer for the suggested time.

A pressure cooker is a good tool for preparing stews and casseroles as it can reduce cooking time by as much as a third.

STIR-FRIES

Cut the meat into thin strips across the grain. This shortens the fibre, making the pieces more tender.

Have the wok or frying pan well heated – searing the meat seals in the juices and makes it cook more quickly. Too low a temperature stews meat in its own juices and toughens it.

To maintain a consistently high temperature, stir-fry meat in a number of small batches.

If stir-frying marinated meat, thoroughly drain off the marinade before cooking meat. Return any reserved marinade to the wok at the end of the cooking time, and bring to a boil just before serving.

PAN-FRIES, BARBECUES AND GRILLS

Have the pan, barbecue, grill or grill plate well heated to ensure meat is sealed. Meat should sizzle immediately when it touches the pan or barbecue, otherwise it will stew and become tough.

When pan-frying and barbecuing, seal the meat on both sides. Beads of juice appearing on the uncooked side indicate the meat is ready to turn. If meat is turned too soon or too often, it becomes dry and tough.

Rare meat only needs to be well sealed. If cooking further, avoid charring by reducing heat after the meat is sealed.

Do not cut into the steak to see if it's cooked. Press the surface with metal tongs; cooked meat will offer some resistance and spring back. It is important to rest the meat a little after cooking to allow the juices to settle. Cutting into a steak before it's done to your liking will allow the juices to escape.

Marinades containing honey or other sugary ingredients burn easily, so it may be necessary to reduce heat immediately after sealing.

glossary

allspice also known as pimento or jamaican pepper; so-named because it tastes like a combination of nutmeg, cumin, clove and cinnamon. Is available whole (a pea-sized dark-brown berry) or ground, and used in both sweet and savoury dishes.

bacon rashers also known as slices of bacon, made from pork side, cured and smoked.

bean sprouts also known as bean shoots; tender new growths of assorted beans and seeds germinated for consumption as sprouts.

bok choy also called pak choi or chinese white cabbage; has a fresh, mild mustard taste and is good braised or in stir-fries. Baby bok choy is also available and is slightly more tender than bok choy.

breadcrumbs

PACKAGED fine-textured, crunchy, purchased white breadcrumbs.

STALE one- or two-day-old bread made into crumbs by grating, blending or processing.

butter use salted or unsalted ("sweet") butter; 125g is equal to one stick of butter.

buttermilk sold alongside all fresh milk products in supermarkets; despite the implication of its name, is low in fat. Originally the liquid left after cream was separated from milk, today, it is commercially made similarly to yogurt.

butternut pumpkin used interchangeably with the word squash, pumpkin is a member of the gourd family used in cooking both as one of many ingredients in a dish or eaten on its own. Various types can be substituted for one another. Butternut is pear-shaped with golden skin and orange flesh.

capers the grey-green buds of a warm climate (usually Mediterranean) shrub, sold either dried and salted or pickled in a vinegar brine. Baby capers, those picked early, are smaller, fuller-flavoured and more expensive than the full-sized ones. Capers should be rinsed well before using.

capsicum also known as bell pepper or, simply, pepper. Native to Central and South America, capsicums come in many colours: red, green, yellow, orange and purplish-black. Be sure to discard seeds and membranes before use.

cardamom native to India and used extensively in its cuisine, this spice can be purchased in pod, seed or ground form.

cayenne pepper a long, thin-fleshed, extremely hot red chilli; usually purchased dried and ground.

cheese

BLUE mould-treated cheeses mottled with blue veining. Varieties include firm and crumbly stilton types to mild, creamy brie-like cheeses.

FONTINA Originating from Italy, fontina is a smooth, firm cheese with a nutty taste and a brown or red rind.

GORGONZOLA Originally from the Lombardy region of Italy, this creamy, cow-milk blue cheese is pierced with needles at about four weeks to encourage the mould to spread.

GOUDA a hard cheese with a creamy texture and nutty flavour. If unavailable, use edam, which is similar but not as creamy.

MOZZARELLA a soft cheese originally from southern Italy where it is traditionally made from water buffalo milk. Having an elastic texture when heated, it is better suited for cooking than for eating on its own.

PECORINO the generic Italian name for cheeses made from sheep milk. Hard, and white-to-pale-yellow in colour, it is made in Italy from the milk of sheep that have grazed on natural pastures.

PIZZA a commercial blend of processed grated mozzarella, cheddar and parmesan.

SWISS generic name for a variety of cheeses originating in Switzerland, among them emmentaler and gruyère.

chillies generally the smaller the chilli, the hotter it is. Use rubber gloves when seeding and chopping fresh chillies to prevent burning your skin.

FLAKES, DRIED deep-red, dehydrated chilli slices and whole seeds; good for use in cooking or as a condiment for sprinkling over cooked foods.

THAI RED also known as "scuds"; small, very hot and bright red; can be substituted with fresh serrano or habanero chillies.

cloves dried flower buds of a tropical tree; can be used whole or in ground form. Has a distinctively pungent and "spicy" scent and flavour.

coconut cream available in cans and cartons; made from coconut and water.

coriander also known as cilantro or chinese parsley; bright-green leafy herb with a pungent flavour. Also sold as seeds, whole or ground.

couscous a fine, grain-like cereal product, originally from North Africa; made from semolina.

crème fraîche a fresh thick cream with a velvety texture and tangy flavour; substitute sour cream if not available.

curry paste some recipes in this book call for commercially prepared pastes of varying strengths and flavours. Use whichever one you feel suits your spice-level tolerance best.

dried shrimp dried salted baby prawns; used as an ingredient in many Asian cuisines.

egg some recipes call for raw or barely cooked eggs; exercise caution if there's a salmonella problem in your area.

eggplant purple-skinned vegetable also known as aubergine. Can be purchased char-grilled, packed in oil, in jars.

fish sauce also called nam pla or nuoc nam; made from pulverised salted fermented fish, most often anchovies. Has a pungent smell and strong taste; use sparingly.

flat-leaf parsley also known as continental parsley or italian parsley.

gai larn also known as gai lum, chinese broccoli and chinese kale, this vegetable is prized more for its stems than coarse leaves. Can be eaten stir-fried on its own or tossed into various soups and noodle dishes.

galangal a rhizome with a hot ginger-citrusy flavour; used similarly to ginger and garlic as a seasoning or an ingredient. Substitute with fresh ginger if unavailable.

garam masala a blend of spices based on varying proportions of cardamom, cinnamon, cloves, coriander, fennel and cumin, roasted and ground together.

ghee clarified butter; with the milk solids removed, this fat can be heated to a high temperature without burning.

ginger also known as green or root ginger; the thick root of a tropical plant.

gnocchi Italian "dumplings" made of potatoes, semolina or flour.

harissa Moroccan sauce or paste made from dried red chillies, garlic, oil and caraway seeds.

horseradish cream a commercially prepared creamy paste made of grated horseradish, vinegar, oil and sugar.

kaffir lime leaves aromatic leaves of a citrus tree; used similarly to bay leaves, usually in Thai cooking.

kalamata olives small, sharp-tasting, brine-cured black olives.

kecap manis also known as ketjap manis; a thick soy sauce with added sugar and spices.

kitchen string made of a natural product such as cotton or hemp so that it neither affects the flavour of the food it's tied around nor melts when heated.

kipfler potato small, finger-shaped potato with a nutty flavour.

kumara Polynesian name of orange-fleshed sweet potato, often confused with yam.

lebanese cucumber short, thin-skinned and slender; also known as the European or burpless cucumber.

lemon grass a tall, lemon-smelling and -tasting grass; the white lower part of the stems are used.

mesclun a salad mixture of assorted young lettuce and other green leaves; sometimes also contains edible flowers.

mince also known as ground meat; we used beef mince unless stated otherwise.

mustard

SEEDS, BLACK also known as brown mustard seeds; more pungent than the yellow (or white) seeds used in most prepared mustards.

WHOLEGRAIN also known as seeded mustard; a coarse-grain mustard made from black and yellow mustard seeds and dijon-style mustard.

noodles

BEAN THREAD also known as bean thread vermicelli, cellophane noodles or glass noodles.

HOKKIEN also known as stir-fry noodles; fresh wheat-flour noodles which slightly resemble thick yellowy-brown spaghetti.

RICE soft white noodles made from rice flour and vegetable oil; available in varying thicknesses, from vermicelli-thin to broad and flat. Rinse under hot water to remove starch and excess oil before using.

oyster sauce made from oysters and their brine, cooked with salt and soy sauce then thickened.

pancetta cured pork belly; bacon can be substituted.

paprika ground dried red capsicum (bell pepper), available sweet or hot.

pide also known as turkish bread. Comes in long (about 45cm) flat loaves as well as individual rounds; made from wheat flour and sprinkled with sesame or black onion seeds.

plum sauce a thick, sweet and sour dipping sauce made from plums, vinegar, sugar, chillies and spices.

polenta also known as cornmeal; a flour-like cereal made of dried corn (maize) sold ground in different textures; also the name of the dish made from it.

preserved lemon a North African speciality, the citrus is preserved, usually whole, in a mixture of salt and lemon juice. Can be rinsed and eaten as is, or added to casseroles and tagines to impart a rich salty-sour acidic flavour.

prosciutto cured, air-dried, pressed ham; usually sold thinly sliced.

redcurrant jelly a preserve made from redcurrants; used as a glaze for desserts and meats, or in sauces.

rice

ARBORIO small, round-grain rice well suited to absorb a large amount of liquid.

BASMATI a white, fragrant long-grain rice which is most usually associated with the food of India.

sambal oelek (also ulek or olek) Indonesian in origin; a salty paste made from ground chillies.

shallots also called French shallots, golden shallots or eschalots; small, brown-skinned, elongated, members of the onion family. Grows in tight clusters similar to garlic.

shrimp paste also known as trasi and blanchan; a strong-scented, almost solid preserved paste made of salted dried shrimp. Used as a pungent flavouring in many South-East Asian soups and sauces.

silverside also known as topside roast; the cut used for making corned beef, usually sold vacuum-sealed in brine.

spring onion vegetable having a small white, walnut-sized bulb, long green leaves and narrow green-leafed tops.

star anise a dried star-shaped fruit of a tree native to China. The pods, which have an astringent aniseed or liquorice flavour, are widely used in the Asian kitchen. Available whole and ground.

tamarind concentrate the commercial distillation of tamarind pulp into a condensed paste. Used straight from the container, with no soaking or straining required; can be diluted with water according to taste.

thai basil has smallish leaves, and sweet licorice/aniseed taste; it is one of the basic flavours that typify Thai cuisine. Available in Asian supermarkets and greengrocers.

tomato sauce also known as ketchup or catsup; a flavoured condiment made from tomatoes, vinegar and spices.

zucchini also known as courgette; small green, yellow or white vegetable belonging to the squash family.

make your own stock

These recipes can be made up to four days ahead and stored, covered, in the refrigerator. Be sure to remove any fat from the surface after the cooled stock has been refrigerated overnight. If the stock is to be kept longer, it is best to freeze it in smaller quantities. *All stock recipes make about 2.5 litres (10 cups).*

Stock is also available in cans or cartons. Stock cubes or powder can be used. As a guide, 1 teaspoon of stock powder or 1 small crumbled stock cube mixed with 1 cup (250ml) water will give a fairly strong stock. Be aware of the salt and fat content of stock cubes and powders and prepared stocks.

BEEF STOCK

2kg meaty beef bones
2 medium onions (300g)
2 sticks celery, chopped
2 medium carrots (250g), chopped
3 bay leaves
2 teaspoons black peppercorns
5 litres (20 cups) water
3 litres (12 cups) water, extra

Place bones and unpeeled chopped onions in baking dish; bake in hot oven about 1 hour or until bones and onions are well browned. Transfer bones and onions to large saucepan, add celery, carrots, bay leaves, peppercorns and water; simmer, uncovered, 3 hours. Add extra water; simmer, uncovered, further 1 hour, strain.

CHICKEN STOCK

2kg chicken bones
2 medium onions (300g), chopped
2 sticks celery, chopped
2 medium carrots (250g), chopped
3 bay leaves
2 teaspoons black peppercorns
5 litres (20 cups) water

Combine ingredients in large saucepan; simmer, uncovered, 2 hours. Strain.

VEGETABLE STOCK

2 large carrots (360g), chopped
2 large parsnips (360g), chopped
4 medium onions (600g), chopped
12 sticks celery, chopped
4 bay leaves
2 teaspoons black peppercorns
6 litres (24 cups) water

Combine ingredients in large saucepan; simmer, uncovered, 1 1/2 hours. Strain.

index

facts & figures

Wherever you live, you'll be able to use our recipes with the help of these easy-to-follow conversions. While these conversions are approximate only, the difference between an exact and the approximate conversion of various liquid and dry measures is minimal and will not affect your cooking results.

dry measures

metric	imperial
15g	1/2oz
30g	1oz
60g	2oz
90g	3oz
125g	4oz (1/4lb)
155g	5oz
185g	6oz
220g	7oz
250g	8oz (1/2lb)
280g	9oz
315g	10oz
345g	11oz
375g	12oz (3/4lb)
410g	13oz
440g	14oz
470g	15oz
500g	16oz (1lb)
750g	24oz (11/2lb)
1kg	32oz (2lb)

oven temperatures

These oven temperatures are only a guide. Always check the manufacturer's manual.

	°C (Celsius)	°F (Fahrenheit)	Gas Mark
Very slow	120	250	1
Slow	150	300	2
Moderately slow	160	325	3
Moderate	180 - 190	350 - 375	4
Moderately hot	200 - 210	400 - 425	5
Hot	220 - 230	450 - 475	6
Very hot	240 - 250	500 - 525	7

liquid measures

metric	imperial
30ml	1 fluid oz
60ml	2 fluid oz
100ml	3 fluid oz
125ml	4 fluid oz
150ml	5 fluid oz (1/4 pint/1 gill)
190ml	6 fluid oz
250ml	8 fluid oz
300ml	10 fluid oz (1/2 pint)
500ml	16 fluid oz
600ml	20 fluid oz (1 pint)
1000ml (1 litre)	13/4 pints

helpful measures

metric	imperial
3mm	1/8in
6mm	1/4in
1cm	1/2in
2cm	3/4in
2.5cm	1in
5cm	2in
6cm	21/2in
8cm	3in
10cm	4in
13cm	5in
15cm	6in
18cm	7in
20cm	8in
23cm	9in
25cm	10in
28cm	11in
30cm	12in (1ft)

measuring equipment

The difference between one country's measuring cups and another's is, at most, within a 2 or 3 teaspoon variance. (For the record, 1 Australian metric measuring cup holds approximately 250ml.) The most accurate way of measuring dry ingredients is to weigh them. When measuring liquids, use a clear glass or plastic jug with the metric markings. (One Australian metric tablespoon holds 20ml; one Australian metric teaspoon holds 5ml.)

If you would like to purchase *The Australian Women's Weekly* Test Kitchen's metric measuring cups and spoons (as approved by Standards Australia), turn to page 120 for details and order coupon. You will receive:

- a graduated set of four cups for measuring dry ingredients, with sizes marked on the cups.
- a graduated set of four spoons for measuring dry and liquid ingredients, with amounts marked on the spoons.

Note: North America, NZ and the UK use 15ml tablespoons. All cup and spoon measurements are level.

We use large eggs having an average weight of 60g.

how to measure

When using graduated metric measuring cups, shake dry ingredients loosely into the appropriate cup. Do not tap the cup on a bench or tightly pack the ingredients unless directed to do so. Level top of measuring cups and measuring spoons with a knife. When measuring liquids, place a clear glass or plastic jug with metric markings on a flat surface to check accuracy at eye level.

Looking after **your interest...**

Keep your ACP cookbooks clean, tidy and within easy reach with slipcovers designed to hold up to 12 books. Plus you can follow our recipes perfectly with a set of accurate measuring cups and spoons, as used by *The Australian Women's Weekly* Test Kitchen.

To order

Mail or fax Photocopy and complete the coupon below and post to ACP Books Reader Offer, ACP Publishing, GPO Box 4967, Sydney NSW 2001, or fax to (02) 9267 4967.

Phone Have your credit card details ready, then phone 136 116 (Mon-Fri, 8.00am-6.00pm; Sat, 8.00am-6.00pm).

Price

Book Holder

Australia: $13.10 (incl. GST).
Elsewhere: $A21.95.

Metric Measuring Set

Australia: $6.50 (incl. GST).
New Zealand: $A8.00.
Elsewhere: $A9.95.

Prices include postage and handling. This offer is available in all countries.

Payment

Australian residents

We accept the credit cards listed on the coupon, money orders and cheques.

Overseas residents

We accept the credit cards listed on the coupon, drafts in $A drawn on an Australian bank, and also British, New Zealand and U.S. cheques in the currency of the country of issue. Credit card charges are at the exchange rate current at the time of payment.

Test Kitchen Staff
Food director *Pamela Clark*
Food editor *Karen Hammial*
Assistant food editor *Amira Ibram*
Test kitchen manager *Kimberley Coverdale*
Senior home economist *Kellie Ann*
Home economists *Belinda Black, Sammie Coryton, Kelly Cruickshanks, Amy Hedges, Cathie Lonnie, Christina Martignago, Jeanette Seamons, Alison Webb*
Editorial coordinator *Laura O'Brien*

ACP Books Staff
Editorial director *Susan Tomnay*
Creative director *Hieu Chi Nguyen*
Senior editor *Julie Collard*
Designer *Mary Keep*
Studio manager *Caryl Wiggins*
Editorial coordinator *Holly van Oyen*
Editorial assistant *Lana Meldrum*
Publishing manager (sales) *Brian Cearnes*
Publishing manager (rights & new projects) *Jane Hazell*
Brand manager *Donna Gianniotis*
Pre-press *Harry Palmer*
Production manager *Carol Currie*
Business manager *Sally Lees*
Chief executive officer *John Alexander*
Group publisher *Jill Baker*
Publisher *Sue Wannan*

Produced by ACP Books, Sydney.
Printed by Dai Nippon Printing in Korea.
Published by ACP Publishing Pty Limited, 54 Park Street, Sydney.
GPO Box 4088, Sydney, NSW 1028.
Ph: (02) 9282 8618 Fax: (02) 9267 9438
acpbooks@acp.com.au
www.acpbooks.com.au
To order books, phone 136 116.
Send recipe enquiries to:
recipeenquiries@acp.com.au
AUSTRALIA: Distributed by Network Services, GPO Box 4088, Sydney, NSW 1028.
Ph: (02) 9282 8777 Fax: (02) 9264 3278
UNITED KINGDOM: Distributed by Australian Consolidated Press (UK), Moulton Park Business Centre, Red House Rd, Moulton Park, Northampton, NN3 6AQ.
Ph: (01604) 497 531 Fax: (01604) 497 533
acpukltd@aol.com
CANADA: Distributed by Whitecap Books Ltd, 351 Lynn Ave, North Vancouver, BC, V7J 2C4.
Ph: (604) 980 9852 Fax: (604) 980 8197
customerservice@whitecap.ca
www.whitecap.ca
NEW ZEALAND: Distributed by Netlink Distribution Company, ACP Media Centre, Cnr Fanshawe and Beaumont Streets, Westhaven, Auckland.
PO Box 47906, Ponsonby, Auckland, NZ.
Ph: (9) 366 9966 ask@ndcnz.co.nz

Clark, Pamela.
The Australian Women's Weekly Dinner: Beef.

Includes index.
ISBN 1 86396 302 2
1. Cookery (beef). I. Title.
II. Title: Australian Women's Weekly.
641.662

© ACP Publishing Pty Limited 2003
ABN 18 053 273 546

Photocopy and complete coupon below

☐ **Book Holder**

☐ **Metric Measuring Set**
   Please indicate number(s) required.

Mr/Mrs/Ms _____

Address _____

_____

Postcode _____ Country _____

Ph: Business hours (   ) _____

I enclose my cheque/money order for $ _____ payable to ACP Publishing.

OR: please charge my

☐ Bankcard   ☐ Visa   ☐ Mastercard
☐ Diners Club   ☐ American Express

Card number

Expiry date ____ /____

Cardholder's signature _____

Please allow up to 30 days delivery within Australia. Allow up to 6 weeks for overseas deliveries. Both offers expire 31/12/04. HLDB03